Ten

Reformed

Doctrines

Simply

Explained

Ten Reformed Doctrines Simply Explained

...by an ordinary pastor using everyday English

Mitchell A. Persaud

New Horizon Publishing
4 Littleborough Crt. Scarborough, ON. M1C4S6

Cover Design: Ashley Zekveld
Editor: Justin Kane

First Printing 2018

Special thanks to all those who encouraged me to complete this work and to those who helped to correct my sometimes-inarticulate language and grammar. Among those who helped were Anco Farenhorst, Rachel Sissons, and my very helpful editor, Justin Kane. I would like to thank my wife Shabeeda, and children Joshua, Joel, Karis, and Annabelle for giving me the freedom to miss some family activities in order to complete this work. I thank my elders for their support and for giving me the time to write. Special thanks to Pastor W. Ralph English, who taught me to care for the flock, Pastor Karl Hubenthal, a true friend, and Pastor Dennis Royall, who challenged me.

May our good God be honored.

Table of Contents

Introduction:

What are Reformation

Doctrines?

Reformation Doctrines Are Historical Doctrines

One of the greatest blessings God has ever poured out on the Church is the sixteenth-century Reformation. Through it, the Gospel of Jesus Christ was recovered, the Bible made widely available, and the worship of God purified. The Reformation began in earnest in 1517. It did not start a new church, and it did not develop new doctrines. It was simply a Reformation of that which had become corrupted.

The Reformation caused people to return to the true Church by leaving the Roman Catholic Church (RCC), which had become corrupted with unbiblical worship and doctrine. There were always true churches that remained faithful to the Gospel truth, churches who were never corrupted by the RCC. The true Church survived in many of the mountain regions of Europe during the centuries when the RCC was growing corrupt and distant from the truth.

But do not assume that because the RCC was so corrupt at the time of the Reformation that it was always that way. Far from it! The

RCC changed over time from being a biblical church, becoming a corrupt beast, even sometimes condemning Christians to be burned at the stake. The Reformers saw the serious heresies of the RCC and called it the "Synagogue of Satan." While the RCC fought desperately against being reformed, the Reformers worked tirelessly to restore the historical doctrines of the Bible and the early Church.

It would be impossible to find truly new doctrines that arose during the time of the Reformation. The major Reformers were always quoting older writers, especially the early Church fathers. Sometimes they even quoted from godly Roman Catholic scholars. You can find in the writings of any Reformer like John Calvin, men like Augustine and Jerome being quoted among many others who lived more than a thousand years before the Reformation. Augustine and Jerome are both widely considered to be Roman Catholic theologians.

Reformation Doctrines and God's Glory

The doctrines from the Reformation consistently center on God's glory. As you study the Reformed doctrines, you will see that there is no promotion of man or his intellect. In fact, in reflection of the Scriptures, Reformation theology clearly denounces the attempt by man to try to reflect his own inventions in worship and life. We will see this in more detail in later chapters.

Further, the scholars of the Reformation were not egomaniacs. They did not name organizations or ministries after themselves as is often done today. **There was never a "John Calvin Ministries**." There was never a "John Knox Organization." Instead, there is a noticeable promotion of God's glory among the Reformers.

The Reformers used a Latin expression to capture this idea: *Soli Deo Gloria*. This is one of the 5 main expressions that came out of the Reformation; it means "solely for the glory of God." In the other 4 key expressions you will see there is little room for the promotion of man—rather, there is a distinct focus on God:

- *Sola Scriptura* means "Scripture alone"—what God says is the ultimate authority in the Church.
- *Sola Fide* means "faith alone"—God saves us through faith alone, apart from works.
- *Sola Gratia* means "grace alone"—God saves us by grace alone, by his decision, not ours.
- *Solus Christus* means "Christ alone"—Jesus is the only Savior and Advocate we have.

The Scriptures, faith, and grace are all gifts of God. None of these things has its origins in man but are from Christ alone. How praiseworthy! How good God is to his children. He gives man everything he needs for his salvation and for his sanctification, (sanctification refers to man's separation from sin and his growth in grace.)

A child was asked by a neighbor: "What is the difference between Reformation theology and Pentecostal theology?" The child's response captured the truth: "**Reformation theology is more God-glorifying.**" So, I lay this out as a challenge to you, dear reader. Read on to see if this is not the truth. If this is God's truth, embrace it and give God the glory.

Reformation Doctrines Are Grounded in the Scriptures

Yes, any Christian will claim that the doctrines of his belief system are grounded in the Scriptures but sometimes a doctrine might only be supported by one verse that could be interpreted in different ways, or the interpretation of that verse is inconsistent with other, clearer verses. At other times some doctrines are only supported by tradition or strong personal feelings, not by the Word of God.

Let me illustrate this. Here we see the Lord's example of humility and service when he washed the disciples' feet. Some churches therefore teach that we also ought to literally wash one another's feet. As a young boy I saw this practiced in a Pentecostal church as a sacrament, yet no other part of Scripture teaches this. If this passage were interpreted in light of other passages, we would find that it is a warm, loving example of

Christian humility and service. It was not a mandate to literally wash one another's feet. The Lord wanted Christians to show the fruit of the Holy Spirit in how we ought to serve one another humbly. **We must look carefully and with great suspicion at doctrines that are developed from one passage of Scripture.**

This is the beauty of Reformation theology: the core doctrines are grounded repeatedly and exhaustively in Scripture. We believe that doctrine has to be consistent with all parts of the Bible, both Old and New Testaments.

You will find in this book that I will seek to prove everything from Scripture and I will aim to take all verses in context. This will make it easier for you to have biblical references available quickly for your own use.

Furthermore, Reformation theology is grounded in clear and logical exegesis from the Holy Scriptures. Exegesis means "reading out the meaning," or finding the true meaning of the text, as opposed to forcing a text to say something other than what it means.

Reformation Doctrines Are Time Tested

Reformation doctrine did not start at the Reformation. The Reformers simply restated and clarified earlier historical doctrines, especially those systematized by Christian scholar and minister St. Augustine, whose teachings were believed and taught before the Reformation by men like John Wycliffe and John Hus. The key **Reformation doctrines have been tested and believed throughout history**, and they have not changed, even if they have been made clearer during the course of Church history.

One of the most central Reformation doctrines is that we are justified (made right) in God's sight by faith alone, known as sola fide in the Latin. This doctrine fell into the waste basket of the RCC, but look at God's Word: "Where is boasting then? It is excluded. By what law? Of works? No, but by the law of faith. Therefore we conclude that **a man is justified by faith apart from the deeds of the law**" (Rom 3:27-28).

Sadly, in our day this doctrine is disappearing again, especially from long-established churches. Some have blatantly attacked it and replaced it with a salvation based on morals and good behavior. Other churches may still notice the verses that teach it, but they have subtly set it aside. As faithful students, you must examine the Scriptures. When you do, this doctrine must be raised to prominence again. Justification by faith alone rightly ascribes salvation to God, who gives it to man by grace alone through faith alone. Glory to God for the doctrine of sola fide!

Because the Reformation doctrines are faithful to the Scriptures, these doctrines cannot be changed. I encourage you to make the effort to understand, believe, and live according to these doctrines. This will be for your good and for the glory of God.

Reformation Doctrines Are Imperfect

It might seem strange to assert that Reformation theology[1] is historically verified, that it insists on the glory of God, and that it is fully grounded in the Scriptures, and yet *now* insist that the Reformation's doctrines are imperfect. But this is not strange at all. **No Reformation scholar would have insisted that all doctrinal matters were settled.** In fact, one of the great blessings of the Reformation was the development of Bible-based theological schools where doctrine could be studied in detail.

Even in the 1600's, when the King James Version of the Bible was first published, the translators strongly warned the readers that the King James translation of the Bible was imperfect and would need to be improved, (as you can see in the original preface of the King James Bible.) They knew in their hearts that even with all their skill and good intentions, they would fall short of perfectly reflecting the passages in English. Following the humble example of the King James Bible translators, it would be arrogant and dishonest for anyone to assert that Reformation doctrines are perfect.

---

1. Reformation "doctrines" and Reformation "theology" are the same basic idea for the purposes of this book.

Again, the key here is that you make an effort to understand the doctrines of the Scriptures, which have been repeated in the faithful churches for more than 2000 years! I encourage you to not be satisfied with simply believing what others say, including what I am saying; you must study and diligently compare what a teacher says with what the Bible says. This is what distinguished the Bereans in Acts 17, who would not even take what the Apostle Paul said without checking it with the previous Scriptures.

We must be like the Bereans:

> Then the brethren immediately sent Paul and Silas away by night to Berea. When they arrived, they went into the synagogue of the Jews. These were more fair-minded than those in Thessalonica, in that they received the word with all readiness, and searched the Scriptures daily to find out whether these things were so (Acts 17:10-11).

Because truth is from God, truth will always stand up to examination.

Chapter I

Man's Problem: Totally

Unable to Please God

One of the foundational doctrines that returned to the Church during the time of the Reformation was the doctrine of man's total inability to do what is truly good in God's sight. So, let's begin by examining this doctrine.

Definition of Total Inability

"<u>Total inability</u>" <u>is the doctrine that man is totally unable to do anything purely good to please God</u>. The term total inability avoids the confusion of the classical Reformed term "**total depravity**," which may make some people think that man is as bad as he could be. **But men and women are not as wicked as we could possibly be**. (There would be absolute chaos in the world if we were!) We are corrupt from the very core of our being, throughout the extent of our being, and therefore totally unable to do anything purely good or pleasing in God's sight.

Man's Total Inability to Do a Truly Good Work

The first thing we must do to prove man's total inability to please God (and earn his salvation) is to show that **man can do nothing truly good in God's sight**.

Most people think of themselves as good, but the Bible teaches that men, women, boys and girls are sinful throughout their being, and totally unable to do what is good in God's sight. Our souls are totally corrupt. **Not one human by himself wants to find God and serve him**. Even more, **there is no one who is able to look for God**. Man lost that ability to do good when he fell into sin in the Garden of Eden. We always want to do what satisfies our own lusts. Even when we are serving others there is always a part of it that is self-serving. Sin has corrupted our hearts so that nothing we do is pure like it should be.

The fact that no one can do any truly, purely good work might seem outrageous to you, or even to most people, so allow me to prove this point based on God's Word.

Why No Man Can do Good Works

For a work to be good, we must do it through faith in Jesus Christ (Rom 14:23b). True faith is a deep-rooted assurance that the Holy Spirit works in us through the Gospel of Jesus. This faith makes us able to receive the forgiveness of our sins. Only the man whose sins are forgiven can do good works to please God.

We may teach our children the truth about creation, the fall of man, and how they can be saved. We might even provide well for our families and go to war to protect them, but if we do not do these things because we have faith in Jesus Christ, none of these actions is truly good in God's sight. God accepts nothing from us unless we come through Jesus Christ. Why? Without faith in Jesus Christ we are enemies of God. Why would God want to reward his enemies? In our prayers we often close with "in Jesus name we pray, Amen." We do this knowing that our prayers are heard because we are God's children through faith in Jesus Christ.

The Scripture says, "**without faith it is impossible to please Him**, for he who comes to God must believe that He is, and that He is a rewarder of those who diligently seek Him" (Heb 11:6). The writer of Hebrews does not say that it is hard to please God without faith; he says it is impossible. Consider Jesus's words directly: "I am the vine, you are the branches. He who abides in Me, and I in him, bears much fruit; for **without Me you can do nothing**" (John 15:5).

Let me illustrate this point. Jesus taught us that we cannot bear good fruit, or show good works, unless we are part of him, the True Vine, and we can only be part of the vine by faith. When Jesus said that we cannot do anything without him, he meant that we cannot do anything "good" without him. We naturally do evil works without having faith in him. The Scriptures are filled with proof of this truth. In Isaiah 29:13, the Lord says, "these people draw near with their mouths and **honor Me with their lips, but have removed their hearts far from Me**." Through Isaiah, God was rebuking the Jews because they pretended to do good without having the right heart—a heart of faith in the coming Savior—to do good works. Further, the Lord Jesus himself rebuked those who were more interested in ritual washing and eating, rather than obedience that comes out of the heart. Only through faith in Jesus Christ are we perfectly cleansed. Only through faith in him can we do truly good works.

Look again at Jesus's words: "Do you not yet understand that whatever enters the mouth goes into the stomach and is eliminated? But those things which proceed out of the mouth come from the heart, and they defile a man. **For out of the heart proceed evil thoughts, murders, adulteries, fornications, thefts, false witness, blasphemies**" (Matt 15:17-19).

So even the most splendid thing we could ever do, maybe saving someone's life or giving wise counsel to those in trouble, or something as small as shoveling snow from an old lady's driveway, if we do not do it from faith in Jesus Christ, then it is not a good work. God would reject that good work and charge it to us as a sin. It becomes a sin to us because we are trying to improperly please God. Talk about total inability to do good!   **For a work to be good, we must do it according to**

Man's Problem: Totally Unable to Please God

Jesus Christ's law. In the Sermon on the Mount (Matthew 5-7), Jesus rebuked the Jewish leaders for doing their work from legalism and formalism, rather than according to the true meaning of the law. "Legalism" is following the letter of the law but ignoring the spirit or intention of the law. "Formalism" is having the outward form of obedience to the law, but not having the right heart in obeying it. The Pharisees loved legalism and formalism, and they fooled people into thinking that they could please God with their pretend good works.

In short, for a work to be good it has to be done according to the right spirit or intention of God's law. So, if we talk nicely to our neighbor but hate him in the heart, our "nice" talk is not a good work. Rather, our "nice" work is hypocrisy. God would not accept it as good. **<u>Yes, we are totally unable to do anything good!</u>** In Matthew 5:20, Jesus teaches "unless your righteousness exceeds the righteousness of the scribes and Pharisees, **you will by no means enter the kingdom of heaven.**" Since we have no righteousness of our own, we need Christ's righteousness counted as ours.

For a work to be good, we must do it for the glory of Jesus Christ. If we care for our aged parents because we want our parents to praise us, rather than doing it for the glory of Jesus Christ, God will hold that work against us as an evil work. We may even make our parents think we are good, but we don't fool God by a "fake" good work. Look how the Scriptures teach that our good works are for the glory of Jesus.

- Matthew 5:16, "Let your light so shine before men, **that they may see your good works and glorify your Father in heaven.**"
- 1 Corinthians 10:31, "Therefore, whether you eat or drink, or whatever you do, <u>do all to the glory of God.</u>"
- 1 Peter 2:12, "having your conduct honorable among the Gentiles, that when they speak against you as evildoers, they may, **by your good works which they observe, glorify God in the day of visitation.**"

Based on these truths, those who do not believe in Jesus Christ cannot do anything truly good. The world may call their work good, but God doesn't. Not a single non-believer can meet God's high criteria for a good work.

The Diagnosis of Man's Condition

We are sinful from before birth, and throughout our being. The Apostle Paul argued that our sins are passed on from every single parent to every single child. He did not say that man merely inherits sinful tendencies. He said that all have sinned, every single person, young and old, saying "just as through one man sin entered the world, and death through sin, and thus death spread to all men, because all sinned" (Rom 5:12).

Examining the sinfulness of man is not a popular idea. It is distasteful to most people because the full nature of our sinfulness can be difficult to accept. Being a missionary, I have been asked "why do you talk so much about sin, and why do you call us sinners?" My answer is simple: **"unless we see the fullness of our sinfulness we will never see the need for the Savior. If we do not see the need for the Savior we will die in our sins and go to hell forever."** Furthermore, if we do not see our sinfulness realistically, from God's perspective, we will treat the work of Christ in a casual way. If we do not see the greatness of our sins, we will never understand the greatness of God's love for us, and we will never be able to worship him as we ought.

> **Unless we see the fullness of our sinfulness we will never see the need for the Savior.**

I like to illustrate it this way. If I have gangrene in my foot I need to know so I can go to the doctor to have my leg cut off. It is not a pleasant thing to have my leg cut off, but I know that gangrene will kill me unless I deal with it in an urgent and aggressive way. If I do not know the danger of gangrene, I might simply end up taking an aspirin, while the disease grows worse.

Even though our pride may be hurt by the knowledge of our sinfulness, it is better to have our pride hurt than for our souls to be sent to hell for eternity. We should not run the risk of misdiagnosis for our condition; that would be eternally deadly. Yet, misdiagnosis of our condition is common because we like having a high self-evaluation. Humans tend to always think highly of ourselves. Pride and conceit are in our hearts. We therefore think we are far more morally righteous than we actually are. We must let the God who created us diagnose our condition—no one could do it better.

Now let us trust the Lord's diagnosis, and examine more of those passages that deal with man's true sinfulness. The Apostle Paul quoted an Old Testament passage (Psalm 14:2-3) to prove this point:

> As it is written: 'There is none righteous, no, not one;
> There is none who understands; There is none who seeks
> after God. They have all turned aside; They have together
> become unprofitable; There is none who does good, no,
> not one.' 'Their throat is an open tomb; With their
> tongues they have practiced deceit'; 'The poison of asps is
> under their lips'; 'Whose mouth is full of cursing and
> bitterness.' 'Their feet are swift to shed blood;
> Destruction and misery are in their ways; And the way of
> peace they have not known.' 'There is no fear of God
> before their eyes' (Rom 3:10-18).

Romans 3 does not allow for the smallest possibility of man's natural ability to please God. One popular way of expressing this is "**we are not sinners because we sin, we sin because we are sinners**." The point is that we have had a sinful nature from the time we were in our mothers' wombs. Furthermore, man is dead to God. Man is blind to God. Man is deaf to God. Look at how King David described himself: "Behold, I was brought forth in iniquity, and in sin my mother conceived me" (Psa 51:5).

The biblical passages are consistent in showing that no man by himself can do good works to please God, and therefore he cannot believe in God or his good news about Jesus. Ponder these passages:

- Romans 3:23, "for all have sinned and fall short of the glory of God;"
- Ecclesiastes 7:20, "there is not a just man on earth who does good and does not sin;"
- Isaiah 59:7-8 "Their feet run to evil, and they make haste to shed innocent blood; their thoughts are thoughts of iniquity; wasting and destruction are in their paths. The way of peace they have not known, and there is no justice in their ways; they have made themselves crooked paths; whoever takes that way shall not know peace;"
- Ephesians 2:1-3, "And you He made alive, who were dead in trespasses and sins, in which you once walked according to the course of this world, according to the prince of the power of the air, the spirit who now works in the sons of disobedience, among whom also we all once conducted ourselves in the lusts of our flesh, fulfilling the desires of the flesh and of the mind, and were by nature children of wrath, just as the others;"
- Romans 8:7-8, "the carnal mind is enmity against God; for it is not subject to the law of God, nor indeed can be. So then, those who are in the flesh cannot please God."

Whether it is our sweet grandma or our best friend who is not a Christian, all are guilty before God and spiritually dead. Someone may be a sincere follower of a different religion, but he is spiritually dead apart from faith in Christ. This guilt places him under God's condemnation. **Man is so wicked that God gave him a new name. God called wicked men "sons of disobedience**." We are not in a neutral position before God. We are the clear enemies of God.

And if this weren't bad enough news, **we are not only enemies of God, we are helpless enemies**. We hate God. Because love is lacking, we cannot truly obey God. Do you see how high God's standards are and how far we fall short? The best works that we can offer to God are like filthy rags. Our good works that we do apart from faith in Jesus are unclean, good for nothing, and only fit to be tossed out. Isaiah confesses "we are all like an unclean thing, and **all our righteousnesses**

are like filthy rags; we all fade as a leaf, and our iniquities, like the wind, have taken us away" (Isa 64:6). How can anyone offer a polluted thing to God and expect to receive God's favor from it? God is not pleased with filthy rags. God will reject man's works!

How Man Became So Bad

We became sinful in two ways. **First, we inherited the sin of Adam and became corrupt**. Adam was the representative of all of us (also called our "federal head"), spiritually and physically, so when he sinned he caused all of us, his offspring, to become sinful. Adam did not merely cause us to have the desire to sin. Adam caused all of us to come under the condemnation of God. We are under eternal condemnation because we are Adam's children. Someone put it well: "What was in the root came up in the shoot." God does not condemn potential sinners. He condemns real sinners. Look again at Romans 5:12: "Therefore, just as through one man sin entered the world, and death through sin, and thus death spread to all men, because all sinned."

Adam's sins were counted as ours. This is called the imputation of sin. That means that Adam's sins were put to our account. At the same time, we must notice that similarly, Jesus Christ's righteousness and holiness are imputed to our account as well, if we believe in him. His life of obedience is credited by God to our account *as if* we perfectly obeyed all his laws, and *as if* we took the punishment for our own sins.

We can understand this representative idea (also called federal head) from Hebrews 7:10, where the Bible says that Levi was in Abraham's loins when Abraham met Melchizedek and tithed to him. Levi was not born yet, but he was considered to have tithed to Melchizedek. Just the same, we were in our first father, Adam. It is true that when we were babies we might not have consciously sinned, but we were considered to have sin in us because we inherited sin from our parents. This is why David wrote that he was sinful even before his brain could think. He said that he was conceived in sin (Psa 51:5). One of Job's companions spoke about the sinfulness of anyone that comes from a woman's body, saying "what is man, that he could be pure? And he who is born of a woman, that he could be righteous?" (Job 15:14).

Second, we become more sinful by our actual sins. These are the sins we commit every day and night that we live. When a baby grows to become conscious of his sinful desires, he begins adding to his guilt daily. Jeremiah wrote in superlative terms to express the degree of man's sinfulness in life. He went back to the source of sin, man's heart, saying "the heart is deceitful above all things, and desperately wicked; who can know it?" (Jer 17:9).

The Apostle Paul argued that the one without faith in Jesus Christ is in a defiled condition: "to the pure all things are pure, but to those who are defiled and unbelieving nothing is pure; but even their mind and conscience are defiled" (Tit 1:15).

Do you see how bad you look before God? God's Word exposes us for who we really are! But did God create man to be so wicked and perverse, unable to do anything good?

The answer to this question is a resounding "no." God created man good for his praise and glory. If we do not see how perfect we were when God created us, we will never understand the greatness of our fall. Have you ever reflected on the perfect state in which we were created?

- Genesis 1:27, "So God created man in His own image; in the image of God He created him; male and female He created them."
- Genesis 1:31, "Then God saw everything that He had made, and indeed it was very good. So the evening and the morning were the sixth day."

Our first parents were perfect in every way. Our first parents were given a perfect place to live, with perfect work. They were able to fully enjoy all the bounties of God's creation. They had everything they needed; therefore, we must conclude that without salvation in Jesus Christ we are regressing from our parents' first state. We are not getting better, even though we experience so much scientific and technological progress in the world today.

Now look back at Genesis 1:27. God created us "good." But this was not some generic "good." This was a spiritual

classification. And God repeated it for emphasis. The fact that we were created in the image of God means that we had certain characteristics of God in us, characteristics that God could give to us. For example, Adam and Eve were holy, loving, and just. Adam and Eve were created with the ability to keep God's law. Of all of God's creation, only man was said to have been created in God's image.

Is Man as Sinful as He Could Be Since He Can Do Nothing Good?

We are sinful in the extent of our being, and we are sinful from the core of our being, but we are not as sinful as we could be—God restrains us. Unrestrained evil would make life unlivable for Christians. Without God's restraint on human sin, terrorists would always win and criminals would control the streets. God gives a number of illustrations of his limiting restraints on the wicked. For example, when the devil wanted to destroy Job, he could not. God had put a hedge around him which Satan complained about, saying "have You not **made a hedge around him**, around his household, and around all that he has on every side? You have blessed the work of his hands, and his possessions have increased in the land" (Job 1:10).

We also find in many of the Psalms of cursing (imprecatory Psalms), that God limited the wickedness of those who were bent on destroying his people. The Psalmists described God as crushing the wicked like clay pots. Zechariah 2:5 speaks of a wall of fire around God's people, much like the pillar of fire that limited the evil of the Egyptians as they charged after the Israelites as they were about to cross the Red Sea. They could not come near the Israelites, however badly they wanted to capture them, because the Lord was a wall of protecting fire (Ex 14). God's restrictions on Egypt were true and necessary.
Shouldn't we thank God that he doesn't allow wickedness to go unchecked?

Errors Refuted: Man's Total Inability

Let's examine some common errors regarding the doctrine of man's total inability to do good, and show what God's Word really teaches.

- Error: People are sick in sin, not fully dead in sin.

Arminians[1] which include Pentecostals, Charismatics, some Baptists, and some other groups, believe that man is not totally dead in trespasses and sin, but rather sick in sin. Being only sick, man still maintains some ability to desire and to perform good works. Yet the Bible teaches that the whole man was affected by sin: his body, his soul, his will, and his mind. So man can't do anything good. **The Bible teaches that man is dead in sin; he is not sick needing medicine, he is dead, needing resurrection.** Look at Ephesians 2:4-5, "But God, who is rich in mercy, because of His great love with which He loved us, even when we were dead in trespasses, made us alive together with Christ (by grace you have been saved)."

Even the desire to do what is truly good has been lost. God must resurrect and pull us towards himself before we will come to him.

- Error: Man was created in a neutral state and his will continues to be free to choose Jesus Christ.

Arminians reject the fact that man was created in true righteousness and holiness. They believe that Adam and Eve were given the power to be good, and that goodness, righteousness, and holiness were not attached to Adam's will when he was created. Therefore, when Adam fell, his will to be good, righteous, and holy was not destroyed. So, the Arminian says, man retains the ability to choose to be good, righteous, and holy. They believe that man was somewhat disabled in his free will, and that man only has a tendency to sin. That is not what the Bible teaches. Look again at Genesis 1:27: "So God created man in His own image; in the image of God He created him; male and female He created them."

---

1. Followers of Jacob Arminius, a seventeenth-century Dutch theologian.

Being "created in God's image" means that Adam and Eve were holy, loving, and just. Having the image of God was not some abstract characteristic. Having the image of God meant that they were able to know and do what was good. God made everything "good," including man (Gen 1:31).

What distinguished Adam and Eve from animals was that animals had no moral framework, while Adam and Eve did. Animals were neutral. Animals had no conscience. But Adam and Eve were moral creatures with living souls. Consider these passages that show man was not morally neutral at creation.

- Colossians 3:8-10, "But now you yourselves are to put off all these: anger, wrath, malice, blasphemy, filthy language out of your mouth. Do not lie to one another, since you have put off the old man with his deeds, and have **put on the new man who is renewed in knowledge according to the image of Him who created him.**"

Here Paul teaches that we have to be re-created to be good again. Our corrupted wills are renewed through Jesus Christ. We must put off wickedness that was naturally there and then put on the works of Christ—Christ's clothes. There is no inkling of neutrality. We move from darkness to light when we become Christians.

- Ephesians 4:23-24, "and be renewed in the spirit of your mind, and that you put on the new man which was created according to God, in true righteousness and holiness.

Even Adam and Eve had to be renewed because they had become corrupted at their roots. Back in the Garden of Eden, every good thing that Adam and Eve needed, God gave to them. There was nothing that was necessary for their work that God did not give to them. It was only when they were drawn away by their own lust for power and physical satisfaction by the devil himself that they sinned against God and fell from that state of perfection. They were no longer able to do truly good works. The image of God in them was damaged. Their consciences were darkened, and their wills were corrupted. The morally good became morally corrupt and bankrupt.

Today we see the promotion of self-esteem everywhere. Because of this, most people are offended that God describes us as sinful and unable to choose Jesus Christ by our own will. But no man by himself will ever choose to repent of his sins and to love Jesus Christ. He will always reject looking to Jesus for salvation. His choice is always sinful. We need to be renewed and reborn before we can choose God. God must move us first.

- Error: Children are not sinful; they become sinful because of bad social influences.

Some people argue that children only sin because they learn to imitate those who are around them. This is a true statement, and it is a lie. **It is true children learn to imitate the sins of their parents, brothers or sisters. But it is a lie to say that children are sinful** *only* **because they are imitating other people's sins.** This denies that children are sinful from conception. It denies original sin.

Arminians believe in original sin in a way, but not as the Bible teaches it. They believe that though you can call Adam's sin the original sin, that original sin is not inherited. They do not see Adam as that real federal, or covenant head of all of God's creation. They do not believe that man is condemned by an inherited sinful nature. They believe that man was condemned because he failed to obey by his own actions. Therefore, many Arminians teach that all children who die will go to heaven.

On the other hand, the Bible teaches that children are born corrupt and are properly called "children of wrath" (Eph 2:3). We are children of wrath because Adam was our representative, and we receive the consequences of his actions. We are children of wrath because we are his natural, physical descendants, and we inherit his sinfulness when we are conceived. This sinfulness is evident from infancy.

- Psalms 58:3, "The wicked are estranged from the womb; they go astray as soon as they are born, speaking lies."
- Psalm 51:5, "Behold, I was brought forth in iniquity, and in sin my mother conceived me."

And each day we add to what we inherited by our sins in thought, word, and action. Apostle Paul in Romans 5:12, says that men died because men sinned in Adam. We are therefore sentenced to die for who we are in Adam.

- Error: Man is not really that bad.

The Bible teaches we are not as sinful as we could be. But is this because man is not inherently bad? No. **God simply limits our ability to do evil**. God limited the evil of Mao, Stalin, Idi Amin, Hitler, Bin Laden, and every other evil leader. The Bible teaches that we are sinful in extent, meaning that we are sinful in all areas of our lives, but we are not as sinful we could be. Consider how God limited the ability of Nebuchadnezzar, that greatest Babylonian king, so he could not cause more damage to God's people. God made him live like wild animals for years to break him.

- Daniel 5:20-21, "But when his heart was lifted up, and his spirit was hardened in pride, he was deposed from his kingly throne, and they took his glory from him. Then he was driven from the sons of men, his heart was made like the beasts, and his dwelling was with the wild donkeys. They fed him with grass like oxen, and his body was wet with the dew of heaven, till he knew that the Most High God rules in the kingdom of men, and appoints over it whomever He chooses."

Though we can say Nebuchadnezzar had a free will, his ability to choose to do right and good was destroyed by his sinful nature. Nebuchadnezzar could only choose to sin. His will was trapped by his sin and not truly free. Now let us look at another well-known verse that reveals man's moral inability.

- Genesis 6:5, "Then the LORD saw that the wickedness of man was great in the earth, and that **every intent of the thoughts of his heart was only evil continually**.

This verse does not teach that we are as sinful as we could possibly be; rather, it teaches that we are prone to always be doing evil to some degree. Remember, we are not permitted by God to be as sinful as we could be. God will limit even Western governments, which are allowing and supporting, by law, many horrible sins like the murder of innocent children, and the destruction of marriage and the family. When God wants change, he will destroy whatever prevents his will from being accomplished, just like he destroyed Pharaoh and gave Israel freedom.

- Exodus 15:1-5, "Then Moses and the children of Israel sang this song to the LORD, and spoke, saying: 'I will sing to the LORD, For He has triumphed gloriously! The horse and its rider He has thrown into the sea! The LORD is my strength and song, And He has become my salvation; He is my God, and I will praise Him; My father's God, and I will exalt Him. The LORD is a man of war; The LORD is His name. Pharaoh's chariots and his army He has cast into the sea; His chosen captains also are drowned in the Red Sea. The depths have covered them; They sank to the bottom like a stone.'"

God stops evil from progressing when it suits his purposes (we cannot always know God's perspective). God's ultimate purpose is that he might be glorified, and that good might come to his people. Sometimes God might be pleased to allow us to experience hardships, but God always has in view that we would love and serve him better when our suffering is finished.

But make no mistake about it, we are corrupt in the whole of our being, through and through. We sin in our hearts, we sin by our words, and we sin through our bodies, and we cannot change by ourselves. We are bad and can only choose to do bad things. **Without faith in Christ, doing things that are considered right and good are still evil in God's sight**. This impossibility of doing truly good things is illustrated in the Bible by the impossibility of a dark-skinned man becoming white, and the impossibility of a leopard losing its spots: "Can the Ethiopian change his skin or the leopard its spots? Then may you also do good who are accustomed to do evil" (Jer 13:23).

- Error: You are only bad if you act out your badness.

Some believe that man only sins by action. This is contrary to the teaching of the Bible. We sin by our thoughts as well. Every evil thought or evil intention is a sin against God. Sins start in the heart. Remember Jesus Christ's words: "For out of the heart proceed evil thoughts, murders, adulteries, fornications, thefts, false witness, blasphemies" (Matt

15:19). Solomon warns us about the heart, saying "Keep your heart with all diligence, for out of it spring the issues of life" (Prov 4:23). And again, Jesus said "A good man out of the good treasure of his heart brings forth good; and an evil man out of the evil treasure of his heart brings forth evil. For out of the abundance of the heart his mouth speaks" (Luke 6:45).

If we have corrupt hearts, evil will come out of them. If we have good hearts, good things will come out of them. Jesus spoke about this in his Sermon on the Mount (Matt 5-7). He said that lust in the heart is a sin. The Apostle Paul taught that covetousness is a sin of the heart. Covetousness is often (and rightly) called the mother of all sins.

- Error: Man would be good if he were educated.

Some think if people were only well educated about right and wrong they would be morally better. Based on this, they reject the teaching of man's total inability to do good. **The Bible does teach that man has some sense of what he should do and not do, and yet he does not do what he should, and he does what he should not.** The Apostle Paul proves this from Romans 2:14, "for when Gentiles, who do not have the law, by nature do the things in the law, these, although not having the law, are a law to themselves."

He taught that everyone has some sense of the law of God in him. The light of nature tells everyone there is a God. **This same light of nature in his conscience make him know that murder is wrong**. Yet that does not stop him from murdering. He simply closes his eyes to God's truth.

Of course, the light that remains in man, and what he sees of God in nature is insufficient to lead him to Christ. He knows God exists, but he does not know how to find God. God must reveal himself in his Word. And even though man is not able to find God through this dim light in him and the evidence of creation, yet man is left without an excuse. He is left without an excuse because man is condemned by his inherited sin in Adam, and he is condemned for his personal sins. **God is clear of fault in all of this as he is under no obligation to tell anyone of his salvation**. He only does this out of love.

We Need New Hearts

The Reformed faith affirms what the Scriptures teach: we are dead in sin and God must resurrect us by regenerating our hearts. Only after God moves are we able to respond in faith and repentance, which are also gifts that God gives to us. Arminians, on the other hand, say that man must reach out of his own free will and receive those gifts that God offers into his heart. Upon doing this, man can become regenerated. Their teaching is not grounded on the Word of God.

When we believe that we are slaves of sin, unable to do truly good, there is a positive impact on our lives. How?

When we see our sinfulness, we are humbled before God. We realize that there is nothing that we could do to merit our salvation because we were dead in our trespasses and sins. We realize that we did not want to do anything to fix the problem of sin in our lives.

When we see the immensity of our sinfulness we will realize even more what Christ has done for us and we will be able to worship God better.

When we see our sinfulness, we understand why the world is the way it is. We understand why Hitler murdered so many people. We understand why terrorists are involved in and promote terrorism. We understand why our children are rebellious even when they are in their cradles. We realize that it is not simply that the world lacks knowledge, but rather, the world is in flagrant rebellion against God, and refuses to hear the Gospel.

When we see our sinfulness and the sinfulness of the world, we will learn to be more patient in our evangelism of non-believers. We know that the world is simply doing what is natural, and that it takes the work of the Holy Spirit of God to bring them under the submission of Jesus Christ. As my professor used to say: "You can't teach a cat to bark."

Chapter 2

Work of God the Father:

Unconditional Election

Should we panic when we hear words like election, predestination, foreordination, and reprobation?[1] We should not. These words and concepts are used in the Bible so we must not be afraid to use them. In order to grasp Christianity's "deep doctrines," we must be sure that we understand biblical terms like these. These take time and hard work to understand.

But there is a purpose behind studying deep doctrines. When we study them, they will cause us to worship and work more wholeheartedly for the Lord. Those who say they have "no creed but Christ" and avoid diligently studying doctrine will never be able to worship and serve the Lord as they should. On the other hand, those who study, understand, and believe Bible doctrines will be able to worship the Lord better, and to serve him more faithfully. Consider one example of this. **When we understand the wonder of our election from the depths of our sin and misery, which is our topic in this chapter, we will praise God like we never did before!**

---

1. Reprobation means the loss of hope for salvation after death, in eternal hell.

Definition of Election

Election is God's unconditional choice of those people he decided to save through the substitutionary, sacrificial death of his Son. Election is God's sovereign choice, meaning that nothing outside of himself caused him to choose one person and not another; our good or bad deeds are not why he chooses us or not (Rom 9:11).

Why Was Election Necessary?

As we saw in the last chapter, **our sin has destroyed our ability to choose what is truly good.** Election was therefore necessary because after The Fall, man lost the ability to do what God sees as good. Man could therefore never choose to be saved. Before The Fall, Adam was perfect and morally capable of obeying God's laws. He was in no way deficient, but he sinned and fell into a state of sin and misery. His sin caused him to lose the ability and the desire to reach out to God for help. This plight came on all of Adam's natural children because he was the natural and federal head of all mankind. Sin separated man from God. This separation is called spiritual death.

Election was necessary because after The Fall man did not want to be saved. He only wanted to live for the "lust of the flesh, the lust of the eyes, and the pride of life" (1 John 2:16).

When we get a full sense of our own inability and sinfulness, we will see why God had to choose some to be his own—some, not all—to have salvation through Jesus Christ.

When Were We Elected?

Jesus Christ was chosen to redeem the elect before the world began. This means that your election—indeed, God choosing you for salvation—took place before the world began, before you were born, and before you did anything good or bad. This is why we say election was **un**conditional.

Look at what the Apostle Peter said about Christ being chosen for us, to be our Redeemer:

> You were not redeemed with corruptible things, like silver or gold . . . but with the precious blood of Christ, as of a lamb without blemish and without spot. He indeed was **foreordained before the foundation of the world,** but was manifest in these last times for you who through Him believe in God, who raised Him from the dead and gave Him glory, so that your faith and hope are in God (1 Pet 1:18-21).

You see, election was not some kind of afterthought in God's mind after man sinned. **Christ's coming was part of the unchangeable counsel and unalterable plan of God,** a God who never changes his mind. This decision by God to save through Jesus Christ some of lost humanity is sometimes called predestination.

Biblical Proofs of God's Unconditional Election

Consider how clearly the Bible speaks of unconditional election:

- Ephesians 1:3-5, "Blessed be the God and Father of our Lord Jesus Christ, who . . . chose us in Him before the foundation of the world, that we should be holy and without blame before Him in love, having predestined us to adoption as sons by Jesus Christ to Himself, according to the good pleasure of His will."

Notice in this passage who elected us (the Father), when he elected us (before the foundation of the world), and the results of electing us (we will be holy and without blame). **Our election and Christ's work are perfectly linked together.** Paul doesn't stop there:

- Ephesians 1:1, "In Him also we have obtained an inheritance, being predestined according to the purpose of Him who works all things according to the counsel of His will."

Our election is the first link in that golden chain of salvation (Romans 8:30). Election ends in glorification, which means God makes sure our faith does not fail. You can read about this in Ephesians 1: the Father chose us, the Son redeemed us, and the Holy Spirit seals us for eternity. If you are elected, you will be saved, if you are saved, you will be secured.

We can also say that in our election, God was the first mover. Hear what Jesus said:

- John 15:16, "You did not choose Me, but I chose you and appointed you that you should go and bear fruit, and that your fruit should remain, that whatever you ask the Father in My name He may give you."

John 15 proves that man would never and could never move to choose God (total inability). God did not look to see who would be good before he elected them. Look at how the Scriptures speak:

- Revelation 17:8, "The beast that you saw was, and is not, and will ascend out of the bottomless pit and go to perdition. And those who dwell on the earth will marvel, <u>whose names are not written in the Book of Life from the foundation of the world</u>, when they see the beast that was, and is not, and yet is."

The elect's names are the names written in the Book of Life before the foundation of the world. This is consistent with what Jesus taught. The elect were given to him before the world was made, and they were given to him in order that they might believe the Gospel and do good works. We were **not** elected **because** of our good works.

- John 6:37-40 is especially clear, when Jesus says: "All that the Father gives Me will come to Me, and the one who comes to Me I will by no means cast out. For I have come down from heaven, not to do My own will, but the will of Him who sent Me. This is the will of the Father who sent Me, that of all He has given Me I should lose nothing, but should raise it up at the last day. And this is the will of Him who sent Me, that everyone who sees the Son and believes in Him may have everlasting life; and I will raise him up at the last day."

Do you see any uncertainty in this passage? We were given to Christ by his Father in the covenant of redemption (which was made before the world began). The elect are an absolute, definite number. Further, when you see the phrase "by no means" in the Bible, it is an expression of double certainty. It means "never, never." **God will not and cannot**

cast out any of the ones he has given to his Son. They can never be lost. Election is final. What a blessed hope Christians have! God chose us. How much more reason we now have to praise God!

Let us now look to the great high priestly prayer of Jesus Christ, to learn more of election.

- John 17:6-12 "I have manifested Your name to <u>the men whom You have given Me out of the world</u>. They were Yours, <u>You gave them to Me</u>, **and they have kept Your word**. Now they have known that all things which You have given Me are from You. For I have given to them the words which You have given Me; and they have received them, and have known surely that I came forth from You; and they have believed that You sent Me. I pray for them. <u>I do not pray for the world but for those whom You have given Me, for they are Yours. And all Mine are Yours, and Yours are Mine</u>, and I am glorified in them. Now I am no longer in the world, but these are in the world, and I come to You. Holy Father, **keep** <u>through Your name those whom You have given Me</u>, that they may be one as We are. While I was with them in the world, <u>I kept them in Your name</u>. <u>Those whom You gave Me I have kept;</u> **and none of them is lost** except the son of perdition, that the Scripture might be fulfilled.

Jesus repeated that some people were given to him. He had no uncertainty about who would believe or not. He prayed for those the Father had given to him (covenant of redemption), and he refused to pray for those who were not given to him. As God, he knew who were not his and he refused to pray for them, but he guaranteed the spiritual safety of the ones who were given to him. (Of course, we must pray for all men because we don't know who the elect are.)

Consider now the words of the writer of Hebrews. He showed how the elect are preserved: Jesus Christ is the eternal High Priest who will continue to show the Father that he paid for all the sins of the elect.

- Hebrews 7:20-22, "And inasmuch as He was not made priest without an oath (for they have become priests without an oath, but He with an oath by Him who said to Him: "The LORD has sworn and will not relent, 'You are a priest forever according to the order of Melchizedek'"), by so much more Jesus has become a surety of a better covenant."

Christ is the source and surety of the covenant of redemption, the means by which you are elected. In other words, you are elected to be in union with Christ, who never fails or changes. He perfectly saves each of his people. He said, "all that the Father gives Me will come to Me, and the one who comes to Me I will by no means cast out" (John 6:37).

Christ took the place of the sinner, and carried in himself the punishment that rightly belonged to that sinner, so that the sinner would be saved from the penalty of his sins. This is why Christ had to humble himself, take on a human nature, obey and suffer for the sins of his people. Election came at a price because the sinner had to be redeemed by someone greater than he—someone perfectly pure.

This knowledge must humble you as God did not choose you because of anything good in you! God gave the Israelites long ago a very simple reason for their election: "because the LORD loves you" (Deut 7:8a). His love for his people is the only reason he gives for electing us.

Consider Proof of Election to Condemnation

While some were elected to eternal salvation, there are some who were elected to eternal condemnation. They were appointed to this just condemnation before the world began. Look at Romans 9, where Paul says

> But indeed, O man, who are you to reply against God? Will the thing formed say to him who formed it, 'Why have you made me like this?' Does not the potter have power over the clay, from the same lump to make one vessel for honor and another for dishonor? What if God, wanting to show His wrath and to make His power known, endured with much longsuffering the vessels of wrath prepared for destruction, and that He might make known the riches of His glory on the vessels of mercy, which He had prepared beforehand for glory (Rom 9:20-23).

God made some vessels for noble use and some vessels for common use from the same lump of clay. He made Esau and Jacob from the same parents, but **he condemned Esau before Esau was born, and before he had done anything bad.** This showed that Esau was already sinful.

Yet God is not unfair in this condemnation. All men deserve to be condemned. God could justly send all men to hell. God is just. Because of who he is, he must be just. Because men reject him, he is just to send them to hell! God is simply gracious to some who deserve his justice, those whom he elected to everlasting life. You will see more on this as we correct some common errors regarding this doctrine below.

On What is Election Based?

Did God choose men on the basis of their nationality? Did he love whites of North America more than he loves blacks of Africa? It seems that there are more Christians in North America. Does that not mean that God elects more whites? God does not choose men based the color of their skin, their intellectual abilities, or their inherent goodness. No one wanted to choose God. Everyone preferred his own way. So, on what was election based?

First, God Elected Us Because He Loved Us. It Was a Positive Act

Deuteronomy 7:7-8 is worth repeating in full:
The LORD did not set His love on you nor choose you because you were more in number than any other people, for you were the least of all peoples; but because the LORD loves you, and because He would keep the oath which He swore to your fathers, the LORD has brought you out with a mighty hand, and redeemed you from the house of bondage, from the hand of Pharaoh king of Egypt.

We further see God's electing love in the lives of Esau and Jacob. Both were bad, but God loved one, Jacob, and reached out to him. Yet God hated Esau, rejected him, and in doing so treated him justly.

- In Romans 9:11-13 Paul speaks of "(the children not yet being born, nor having done any good or evil, that the purpose of God according to election might stand, not of works but of Him who calls), it was said to her, 'The older shall serve the younger.' As it is written, 'Jacob I have loved, but Esau I have hated.'"

Paul also points out God's electing love in 2 Timothy 1:8-9, saying

Therefore do not be ashamed of the testimony of our Lord, nor of me His prisoner, but share with me in the sufferings for the Gospel according to the power of God, who has saved us and called us with a holy calling, not according to our works, but according to His own purpose and grace which was given to us in Christ Jesus before time began.

Second, God Elected Us in Order That We Would Worship Him

If we take some of the credit for being Christians, our worship will be half-hearted.

Salvation is for the glory of God. In fact, man is called to "do all for the glory of God" (1 Cor 10:31). We are told in 1 Samuel 12:22 that this is God's motive too: "For the LORD will not forsake His people, for His great name's sake, because it has pleased the LORD to make you His people." We bring glory and honor to God when we worship him and work for him. Jesus affirmed this in John 15:16, saying "you did not choose Me, but I chose you and appointed you that you should go and bear fruit, and that your fruit should remain, that whatever you ask the Father in My name He may give you."

Those who reject God's election of man as the foundation of our salvation rob God of the glory that belongs to him. We must give him full credit for what he has done. If we take some of the credit for being Christians, our worship will be half-hearted. Look at how Jonah responded to God's salvation after Jonah did everything he could to run away from the Lord: "but I will sacrifice to You with the voice of thanksgiving; I will pay what I have vowed. Salvation is of the LORD" (Jon 2:9). Jonah rightly understood that he was not the source of his own salvation. What a stark contrast from the doctrine of our Arminian friends. <u>God chose some whom he would redeem in Jesus so they would worship him</u>. To approach God is to come to him in worship. David praised God saying "Blessed is the man You choose, and cause to approach You, that he may dwell in Your courts. We shall be satisfied with the goodness of Your house, of Your holy temple" (Psa 65:4).

Third, God Elected Us to Show His Power

God has the right, as the Creator, to do as he wishes with his creation. In our sin nature, we do not want to believe this or to rejoice in it. Apostle Paul anticipated our objection and answered it:

> You will say to me then, "**Why does He still find fault? For who has resisted His will**?" But indeed, O man, who are you to reply against God? Will the thing formed say to him who formed it, "Why have you made me like this?" Does not the potter have power over the clay, from the same lump to make one vessel for honor and another for dishonor? **What if God, wanting to show His wrath and to make His power known, endured with much longsuffering the vessels of wrath prepared for destruction, and that He might make known the riches of His glory on the vessels of mercy, which He had prepared beforehand for glory, even us whom He called, not of the Jews only, but also of the Gentiles?** (Rom 9:19-23).

Do you see how important this doctrine is? Wouldn't you worship God even more, knowing that you were elected purely from love? Wouldn't you then want to tell others of God's great love and show his power that saved you?

How Does Salvation Come to the Elect of God?

Election is worked out in the elects' lives through the preaching of the holy Gospel—the Good News about Jesus Christ. Jesus is the source of life. He is the vine. He is the olive tree. He must choose to graft his elect in so they can draw from him and live. We can see this happen in Acts 13:48—"now when the Gentiles heard this, they were glad and glorified the word of the Lord. And **as many as had been appointed to eternal life believed**."

Do you see how important it is to preach the Gospel and to support the preaching of the Gospel through the local church, and through missionary work? <u>The elect are not zapped from heaven with the Gospel</u>. We must carefully and persistently preach the Gospel! We must also display the Gospel through the Sacraments, baptism and the Lord's Supper.

Errors Refuted: Unconditional Election

There are some common errors regarding the doctrine of election of which we must become aware and which we must be able to refute.

- Error: God elected us only because he looked ahead and saw that we would have faith.

To answer this error, we must look at the passage that is often (mis)used to try to prove this point:
Romans 8:29-30 says "whom He foreknew, He also predestined to be conformed to the image of His Son, that He might be the firstborn among many brethren. Moreover whom He predestined, these He also called; whom He called, these He also justified; and whom He justified, these He also glorified."

The first part of refuting this is to **remember man is unable to do anything truly good**. Only by God's electing love could any person be saved. God had to begin the work of salvation; we could have never done so ourselves. We were neither willing nor able to do anything truly good and pleasing before God. So, our election couldn't have been based on what we do.

The second part of refuting this error is to ask: Does the Apostle Paul really say that God looked into the future to see who would have faith, electing them in response? No, he didn't. The word "foreknew" simply means "fore-loved." Foreknew speaks of close "experiential" knowledge (love), not a factual knowledge, like $2 + 2 = 4$. In various places in the Bible, "knew" is often used euphemistically (saying something strong in a nice way) for love. For example, Adam "knew" his wife and she conceived. This means he knew her intimately and experientially. He loved her (Gen 4:1).[2] So "foreknowledge" means "to love ahead of time." It does not mean "to know beforehand what someone will do." If we break up words to get their meaning instead of looking at their biblical meaning, we will get into trouble. Remember this old illustration: butterfly is not made up of butter and a fly.

In summary, **since no one can come to faith in Jesus without being awakened (regenerated) by God, and since no one can have faith without it being given by God, then no reasonable person can conclude that God would elect based on foreseen faith**. That would be illogical. Rather, God determined whom he would elect out of love, and he then gave them faith to receive what he offered. This is election.

- Error: No one is ever reprobated; God loves all men.

God hates sinners. David, through the Holy Spirit, said "The boastful shall not stand in Your sight; You hate all workers of iniquity" in Psalm 5:5, and "The Lord tests the righteous, but the wicked and the one who loves violence His soul hates" (Psa 11:5). Apart from Christ, we are all his enemies. This does not mean God does not also have pity for

---

2. You can see "knew" used like this in Num 31:18, Psa 1:6, Am 3:3, Matt 7:23, 2 Tim 2:19, and 1 Cor 8:3.

sinners. Yet since all men naturally hate God and wish to be apart from him, he allows them to become reprobated.

How does reprobation happen? In election God chooses his children, redeems them by the blood of his Son, and seals them by his Holy Spirit for eternity. But in reprobation, God does nothing. He leaves men to their natural state so they continue in their rebellion and self-hardening. You can see this in the life of Pharaoh. God left him alone and his heart became hardened. With no help from God, man naturally hardens himself against God and lives in rebellion (Ex 8:15, 32). When the Bible says that God hardened Pharaoh's heart, Moses was writing as man would see it. But from God's perspective, he only had to leave Pharaoh alone in his sin (Ex 9:12; 10:1, 20, 27; 14:8). Remember, God does not make people sin.

Others argue against this doctrine of reprobation because they think that God is too nice and sweet to reject someone and send him to hell. It seems to them that this is in conflict with God's love. You might hear someone say when an unbeliever dies: "He is with God now." They assume God has chosen and loves every single person the same, and eventually everyone ends up in heaven. Some, like Roman Catholics, believe in purgatory, where the wicked will wait, be purged of remaining sin, and then moved to heaven. The belief in the eternal fires of hell is missing from their beliefs. But look at these scriptural proofs of reprobation. Look how God leaves sinful man and he becomes hardened.

- Romans 1:28, "And even as they did not like to retain God in their knowledge, <u>God gave them over to a debased mind</u>, to do those things which are not fitting."
- Romans 9:11-13, "(for the children not yet being born, nor having done any good or evil, <u>that the purpose of God according to election might stand</u>, not of works but of Him who calls), it was said to her, 'The older shall serve the younger.' As it is written, 'Jacob I have loved, but Esau I have hated.'"

God says that he hated Esau, and he hated Esau before Esau had done anything, even before Esau was born. God justly left him to his own devices. And this was not the first time that God had said this of Esau and his people, the Edomites.

- Malachi 1:2-3, "'I have loved you,' says the LORD. 'Yet you say, "In what way have You loved us?" Was not Esau Jacob's brother?'" Says the LORD. 'Yet Jacob I have loved; But Esau I have hated, and laid waste his mountains and his heritage for the jackals of the wilderness."

There were people that God hated for their evil actions, and he left them in their sin. Now let us consider Jeremiah's words that show God's reprobation and rejection of some. The prophet wrote "people will call them rejected silver, because the LORD has rejected them" (Jer 6:30).

God had the right to reprobate all men because of sin, and it is an act of his great grace that he elected some to everlasting life. Don't miss God's goodness. Don't ignore it. God loved some before they were born, and he chose them and redeemed them through his Son. Be thankful that God loves many!

- Error: if election were true, then I can't be held responsible for my actions.

If election were true, how could man be responsible for what he does? Isn't man a robot? Isn't this fatalism, like Hindus believe? The Apostle Paul anticipated that question from his readers and responded:

What shall we say then? Is there unrighteousness with God? Certainly not! For He says to Moses, "I will have mercy on whomever I will have mercy, and I will have compassion on whomever I will have compassion." So then it is not of him who wills, nor of him who runs, but of God who shows mercy. For the Scripture says to Pharaoh, "For this very purpose I have raised you up, that I may show My power in you, and that My name may be declared in all the earth." Therefore He has mercy on whom He wills, and whom He wills He hardens. You will say to me then, "Why does He still find fault? For who has resisted His will?" But indeed, O man, who are you to reply against God? Will the thing formed say to him who formed it, "Why have you made me like this?" Does not the potter have power over the clay, from the same lump to make one vessel for honor and another for dishonor? What if God, wanting to show His wrath and to make His power known, endured with much longsuffering the vessels of wrath prepared for destruction (Rom 9:14-22).

So, what was Paul's response? He pointed out that we can't fit into our heads how God's sovereignty and man's freedom work together. God is sovereign and we are not robots, but our mind is too feeble to put it together. But because both are taught in the Scriptures (God elects in his sovereignty and man is responsible if he goes to hell), he requires that we believe both. The Apostle Paul never tries to explain these two things. He merely stated them as true and warns us not to question God.

Let us illustrate this point based on the life of the wickedest man to have ever lived: Judas the Betrayer, whom Jesus called "the son of perdition" in John 17:12. Jesus pointed out that this man was reprobate, saying his reprobation happened "that the Scripture might be fulfilled," and so he had no hope of salvation, yet he was one hundred percent responsible for his actions. God had even predicted the reprobation of Judas in Psalms 41 and 109. Peter confirmed similarly: "They stumble, being disobedient to the word, to which they also were appointed" (1 Peter 2:8b).

All the detailed workings of God our Father are infinite, but we always remember the fact that the blood of Christ was shed for the complete remission of all our sins.

- Error: if election were true, God is unfair.

Why doesn't God save all men? Why did he choose some and not others? Isn't God being unfair?

First, God does what he does for his own good pleasure. Election is not primarily about you. Election is about God's love to his chosen people, his saving them to worship him, and displaying his power (which causes men to worship him).

Second, God is fair to those who reject him and who get sent to hell. God can never be accused of being unfair. It is against his nature. He graciously gives gifts to some. Life is his; he gives it to whomever he wills. Jesus thanked the Father that "all things have been delivered to Me by My Father, and no one knows the Son except the Father. Nor does anyone know the Father except the Son, **and the one to whom the Son wills to reveal Him**" (Matt 11:27). Remember, God did not choose us because we were good. For none is good (Rom 3:9-18). All men are in a state of shameful sin, in a sea of guilt, and in total condemnation before a holy God.

After Paul shows how bad our condition in sin is in Romans 3:9-18, he goes on to say, "we know that whatever the law says, it says to those who are under the law, that every mouth may be stopped, and all the world may become guilty before God" (v. 19).

Third, those who think God is unfair often (mis)quote Acts 10:34, which says "Peter opened his mouth and said: 'In truth I perceive that God shows no partiality.'" It seems from a reading of this text that God is impartial to whom he chooses as his own. But make no mistake about it—that is butchering the text to try to prove a point that is not there. This passage was not intended to teach of God's election of one individual over another. Rather, this passage was intended to teach that God does not choose one nation over another. God has his people in all nations, and the Jews were being warned not to find false comforts in the fact that they were God's special people.[3] To prove this point, look at the next verse. This passage was not about election, but about the extent of God's kingdom; watch as Peter goes on: "in every nation whoever fears Him and works righteousness is accepted by Him" (Acts 10:35).

Further, the argument that "if election were true then God is unfair," assumes that we know what "fair" is. But our sense of fairness has been corrupted. For example, many think that because one man has a lot of money, the government should tax him a higher percentage and spread the wealth around to those who have less. (Even some Christians think this is good.) The "unfair share" has been redefined to mean "fair share." Because of sin, man does not even know what fairness is.

But election is true. God is not unfair to any. God is gracious to some.

---

3. Look back at John chapter 3.

- Error: if election were true, then God is the author of sin.

Some argue against election because they think that if election were true then God would be the author of sin. They argue that since God condemned people before they were born, they have no chance to live obedient lives, and therefore God is the cause of their sinfulness.

First, **God is never the cause of sin**. To say that God causes sin is an abominable blasphemy against the Holy One in heaven. James put it this way—"Let no one say when he is tempted, 'I am tempted by God'; for God cannot be tempted by evil, nor does He Himself tempt anyone" (James 1:13).

Second, **God gave man a free choice when he was created**. Man did freely choose to sin against God. Man chose to sin because of his own lust. Was that part of God's plan? Yes. Yet, man's conscious choice to sin was done in such a way that he was fully responsible for his sin so that he could not charge God with causing sin. Both things are true and we must believe them, though we cannot reconcile them in our tiny brains. The Apostle Paul said: "Who are you man to talk back to God?" (Rom 9:20). And this is not only a New Testament doctrine. In Proverbs 16:4, Solomon said "The LORD has made all for Himself, Yes, even the wicked for the day of doom." The Lord in Isaiah said, "I form the light and create darkness, I make peace and create calamity; I, the LORD, do all these things" (45:7). Man is sinful. God is holy.

- Error: If election were true, man would become lazy.

One of the more common objections to the doctrine of election is that man would become lazy and live a self-indulgent life if he knew that God had chosen him.

First, to argue this way is like saying that something is bad because it can be misused. It is like arguing that since 500 people in North America are killed by hammers each year, hammers must be bad, or like saying since people who are fat use spoons, therefore spoons make us fat. But if the doctrine is clearly taught in the Scriptures, we have to accept it. You may not say: "This doctrine will not promote my faithfulness, so I will drop it." You are to labor to believe and obey God's Word at all times.

Second, the elect person will live a life of faithfulness and prove that he is elect. The elect will not be indulgent. The Christian will not "continue in sin that grace may abound" (Rom 6:1). He will consciously labor to prove his election, as Peter commanded: "Therefore, brethren, be even more diligent to make your call and election sure, for if you do these things you will never stumble" (2 Pet 1:10).

- Error: If election were true, preaching is useless

Does the doctrine of God's loving, unconditional election make preaching useless? And if none of the elect will be lost, why bother to preach the Gospel at all?

First, <u>**God uses the preaching of the Gospel to call his elect home**</u>. We can say with the Psalmist that God will open our eyes to see all the wonderful things that he has done for us. So we must preach the Gospel loudly and clearly everywhere, as Jesus commanded in Matthew 28:19-20, where he said "Go therefore and make disciples of all the nations, baptizing them in the name of the Father and of the Son and of the Holy Spirit, teaching them to observe all things that I have commanded you; and lo, I am with you always, even to the end of the age. Amen."

Second, **Jesus came as a preacher himself,** preaching the Good News, and his way was prepared by a preacher, John the Baptist. Election and preaching are both part of God's plan. Paul makes this clear in Romans 10:14-15: "How then shall they call on Him in whom they have not believed? And how shall they believe in Him of whom they have not heard? And how shall they hear without a preacher? And how shall they preach unless they are sent? As it is written: 'How beautiful are the feet of those who preach the Gospel of peace, who bring glad tidings of good things!'"

Since election is worked out in preaching, are you preaching, and do you support the preaching of the holy Gospel?

Election is Grace

God's Word reminds us of the greatness of his love by which he chooses us to be his children. He should have hated everyone, for everyone was corrupted and fought against him. To hate everyone would have been fair. But what great love the Father has for us, his children! "Behold what manner of love the Father has bestowed on us, that we should be called children of God!" (1 John 3:1).

God does not send some deserving sinners to hell, he put their punishment on his own Son. What amazing love! What response then must come from the Christian? Be humble, knowing that our salvation did not depend on us. Be full of praise for what God has done for us. Be diligent in our service to the Lord. Paul makes this clear to us: "Therefore, my beloved, as you have always obeyed, not as in my presence only, but now much more in my absence, work out your own salvation with fear and trembling; for it is God who works in you both to will and to do for His good pleasure" (Phil 2:12-13).

And consider one more thing regarding election. **Don't worry about the salvation of children who die in infancy.** Christians can claim the covenant promises of God that he would save us and our household. Remember, our children are not saved because they are pure, for they inherited Adam's sin. Our children are not saved because they are innocent, for they may have committed sins as infants. They were sinful from the time they were in their mothers' wombs. But if God condemned all children because of Adam's faithlessness without their consent, why could he not save them without their consent, based on the faith of parents? What amazing comfort this is to God's people, especially to those who have lost children in infancy or by miscarriages! What a blessing this doctrine is to those who may have mentally handicapped children!

Jesus said, "no one can come to Me unless it has been granted to him by My Father" (John 6:65). Let this knowledge of our election remove fear from our hearts, for our future is secure. God's work of election is unalterable!

Chapter 3

Work of God the Son: Dying for His Own

The Bible teaches that **Christ's atonement—his sacrifice for sins—was intended for those people God elected** (the subject of the last chapter); Christ's atonement was not for every single person. You see, if Jesus died for all the sins of all men and yet God sent some to hell, God would be unfair and unjust. He would be unfair because he would send some to hell when the price for freedom was already paid. He would be unjust because he would punish two people for the same sin. But God is neither unfair nor unjust. He would not punish Christ for a man's sin and then punish the man as well.

It might be popular to teach that Jesus died for every single person in the world, and it might seem to be inclusive, which is a popular social thing these days, but that is not what the Bible teaches. **Jesus did not die for everyone; he died for his elect only.**

Before we get further into the doctrine, let's start with a definition of "limited" atonement.

Definition of Limited, or Definite Atonement

Limited atonement means that Christ, by his death, will save those whom the Father chose through love before the foundation of the world (Eph 1:4-5).

Sometimes there is confusion with the term "limited atonement." Why? When we say Christ's atonement was limited, some people think we mean that Christ can't save the whole world—that he doesn't have the ability. But that is not what we are saying, and it is definitely not what the Bible teaches. **Christ has the ability to save all men.** The effect of his death was so great that it was sufficient to make substitution for the sins of the whole world, every man, woman, boy, or girl who has ever lived and who will ever live. But just because something is powerful does not mean we will get it. A medicine might be able to cure our infection, and someone may have tons of that medicine, but someone has to give us that medicine to cure our infection. So, in order to avoid confusion of those who might think that we are saying that Jesus is unable to save the whole world, it is better to use the term "definite atonement," rather than "limited atonement." In short, the Lord Jesus came to save a definite number, though he was able to save the whole world.

The best way to understand this doctrine is by looking at the nature of Christ's atonement in general. This will form the foundation to prove definite atonement.

What Does the Bible Teach About Christ's Atonement?

First, the blood of Jesus Christ that was shed on the cross cleanses us from all sins. No other thing can do this. No other person can do this. The Scriptures are abundantly clear on this: "if we walk in the light as He is in the light, we have fellowship with one another, and **the blood of Jesus Christ His Son cleanses us from all sin**" (1 John 1:7); "knowing that you were not redeemed with corruptible things, like silver or gold, from your aimless conduct received by tradition from your

Work of God the Son: Dying for His Own

fathers, but **with the precious blood of Christ**, as of a lamb without blemish and without spot" (1 Peter 1:18-19).

The atonement of Jesus is a free gift, and we are glad that it is. We could not purchase our salvation or bribe our way into heaven. Christ's atonement was sufficient to do the work and make us clean before God, clean from all our sins. This Gospel is expressed in 2 Corinthians 5:21 beautifully: "For He made Him who knew no sin to be sin for us, that we might become the righteousness of God in Him." Paul also spoke of our salvation as a rescue for helpless sinners: "For when we were still without strength, in due time Christ died for the ungodly. For scarcely for a righteous man will one die; yet perhaps for a good man someone would even dare to die. But God demonstrates His own love toward us, in that while we were still sinners, Christ died for us" (Rom 5:6-8).

This means that Muslims, Hindus, Buddhists, atheists, and secular humanists have no hope of pleasing God, and will go to hell for eternity because they are without Jesus's atonement for their sins. Only Christ's atonement will satisfy God's righteous anger against man. There is no forgiveness without sacrifice. (Immediately you should start to see the need for evangelism.)

Second, **all the Old Testament sacrifices for atonement pointed to some aspect of the work of Jesus;** they had no value of themselves. Their value was in what they represented. The priest who offered these sacrifices was forgiven his sin because he offered them by faith in the coming sacrifice of Jesus Christ. The sacrifices of bulls and goats were not the ground of forgiveness. Goat's blood cannot satisfy God's justice (Heb 10:4).

Third, **none of the people of the Old Testament, like Abraham, Moses, David, or Solomon could bring peace with God.** In fact, they had to deal with their own sins. Solomon's name means "peace," but he was a man of many sins who brought trouble to Israel. Even the godly Virgin Mary made it clear that she needed a Savior (Luke 1:47).

Only those who look in faith to Christ's atonement can be saved.

Let's now look at how Christ's atonement was for a definite number, those whom the Father gave him, a number that can never be changed.

Biblical Proofs of Definite Atonement

First, it is impossible that Christ died for all men if all men are not saved. If it were true that Christ died for every single person, then God would be unfair and unjust. No one would dare accuse God of being unfair and unjust.

Second, let's look directly at the Bible now. **There is a definite number—the elect—in whom God works from beginning to end, from the beginning of salvation to the end in heaven.** There is no uncertainty regarding the number of people to be saved. Consider that from before Jesus was born, **the angel told his mother Mary that he would "save His people from their sins" (**Matt 1:21). He would not save all people, as in every single man.

Also, in his high priestly prayer in John 17, **Jesus said that he was not praying for those who were not his, but he only prayed for his people** (v. 9). Jesus even prayed for his people who would believe in the future, but he refused to pray for those who would reject him in the future (v. 20). Jesus further clarified that he did not come to save all people. After all, it was Jesus who said, "this is the will of the Father who sent Me, that of all He has given Me I should lose nothing, but should raise it up at the last day" (John 6:39).

Jesus came to save "his" people, those whom his Father gave to him in the Covenant of Redemption, a covenant made between God the Father and God the Son before the creation of the world. The elect were a gift from God the Father to God the Son (a definite number) and not one of them would be lost. Do you see any uncertainty in Jesus's words in John 6? Look again!

Look also at the certainty in how Jesus speaks of his work on behalf of his sheep: "I am the good shepherd. The good shepherd gives His life for the sheep" (John 10:11). "My sheep hear My voice, and I know them, and they follow Me. And **I give them eternal life, and they** shall never perish; neither shall anyone snatch them out of My hand" (John 10:27-28). Do you see that wonderful promise? Jesus will not only save **his** sheep but he will preserve **his** sheep. Yes, Jesus's death was great enough to save the whole world from its sins, but he died for his people, whose number is unknown to us, but certain to him.

When we see the intention in Christ's atonement, to save his people, we must praise God that the Father elected us and secured our salvation through the sacrifice of Jesus.

The Necessity of the Atonement

The payment of sin is death. All men, women, and children deserve to die, to have their blood spilled. To receive new life, we needed a substitute who would take the full punishment for our sins by having his blood spilled. The author of Hebrews focused on the blood payment for sin: "according to the law almost all things are purified with blood, and **without shedding of blood there is no remission** (9:22). Remission means that our sins are forgiven, removed for good.

This is what Jesus did for us. Other religions teach their followers that they can please their god by their actions. They think highly of themselves and their abilities to please their god, and they have to acknowledge that their god has lower standards than Jehovah God of Israel. The standards of false gods always allow sinful men to reach them by their own efforts. Muslims, for instance, believe that Allah would declare them forgiven if they fulfill the pillars of Islam. One of those pillars is the giving of Zakat—2.5% of their surplus money or goods to others. But for Christians, we would understand God to be unjust and a liar if he said we could earn his favor by our actions, for the Bible teaches us that no man can earn God's favor and freedom by giving money. But God is neither unjust nor a liar. **Sins require death, the shedding of the blood of the guilty.** This is just one of the ways we have absolute certainty that we do not worship the same God as other religions.

It is true that we could take God's justice by going to hell for eternity, but this would mean that we would never be able to have eternal life. God was pleased to accept Jesus who took our punishment as our substitute and was also raised from the dead for us. This is the only means by which we are able to get forgiveness of sins and new life.

The Fullness of the Atonement

The result of Jesus's work is that the Father's anger against us was fully satisfied. **Christ became a curse for us and he drank of the cup of God's wrath for us.** The theological phrase for this is "substitutionary," or "vicarious" atonement.

Isaiah 53, written over 700 years before Jesus died on the cross, is one of the clearest Old Testament prophecies of what the atonement accomplished for us. Isaiah wrote "it pleased the LORD to bruise Him; He has put Him to grief. When You make His soul an offering for sin, He shall see His seed, He shall prolong His days, And the pleasure of the LORD shall prosper in His hand. **He shall see the labor of His soul, and be satisfied**. By His knowledge **My righteous Servant shall justify many, For He shall bear their iniquities**" (Isa 53:10-11).

As a result of Christ's atonement, the Jew and the Gentile will be saved. So whether we are from Africa, China, or the West Indies, the atonement of Christ alone is the basis of our salvation.

<u>**As a result of the atonement, those for whom Christ died can never be lost**</u>. The atonement was the next step in the unbreakable golden chain of salvation. God elected his people and then he saved them by providing the atonement for their sins.

The golden chain is found in Romans 8:28-30—
And we know that all things work together for good to those who love God, to those who are the called according to His purpose. For whom He foreknew, He also predestined to be conformed to the image of His Son, that He might be the firstborn among many brethren. Moreover whom He predestined, these He also called; whom He called, these He also justified; and whom He justified, these He also glorified.

How Do We Get That Atonement?

If we receive by faith the atonement of Jesus as our own and we ask God to count his death as ours, we are saved. After all, Christ fully propitiated God's anger, and he fully expiated for our sins. Propitiation is the satisfying of God's anger against us. Expiation is a covering for our sins. We are therefore fully reconciled to his Father. Our ability to believe comes from God. It is a gift. It is not in us. It is not natural. We are natural rebels without God. Look at proof of this gift from God. **We are granted the ability to believe, as well as the desire to do so**.

Paul makes this crystal clear in Philippians 1:29, "For to you **it has been granted** on behalf of Christ, not only **to believe in Him**, but also to suffer for His sake."

There is no other way to be saved than by grace alone, through faith alone, and in Jesus Christ alone. Someone might be really nice, generous, and an all-round good person, but he is not saved except through receiving Christ's atonement by grace through faith. Grace is God's unearned favor to us, and faith is the empty hands we are given to receive what Jesus accomplished for us. Someone could give large sums of money to charity, help orphans around the world, dig wells, build hospitals for the poor, and improve living conditions for the poor around the world, but without Christ's atonement for him, he will go to hell. Man is only changed by Jesus Christ. This is why the disciples were commanded to go to every part of the world to preach the Gospel of Jesus Christ so the nations could receive the benefits of Christ's atonement.

We too must take the message of Christ's vicarious atonement to a lost world.

Errors Refuted: The Atonement

Many people find the doctrine of definite atonement repulsive and so reject it quite strongly. So let's highlight some of the more common errors that some hold and answer their arguments. Maybe you have been taught some of these errors.

- Error: The atonement was altogether not really necessary.

There are some liberal pastors who believe and teach that Christ's atonement for sins was not really necessary for salvation. They believe that Christ came to set a good moral example for others to follow. And further, they believe that if Jesus did die, it was simply a reminder that you must be willing to sacrifice your time, money, and energy for the good of other people. In other words, his death was an example for you to follow.

But Christ did not die simply to set a good example of self-sacrifice that people must imitate today. Yes, Christ was a good example, but that was not why he came.[1] Christ died as a substitutionary atonement to satisfy God's great anger against wretched sinners.

Hebrews 9:12 - Not with the blood of goats and calves, but with His own blood He entered the Most Holy Place once for all, having obtained eternal redemption.

Hebrews 9:26 - He then would have had to suffer often since the foundation of the world; but now, once at the end of the ages, He has appeared to put away sin by the sacrifice of Himself.

There was no uncertainty about what he accomplished when he died on the cross. Consider one more passage to flesh out the idea of the sacrifice of Christ for you: "Christ has redeemed us from the curse of the law, having become a curse for us (for it is written, 'Cursed is everyone who hangs on a tree'), that the blessing of Abraham might come upon the Gentiles in Christ Jesus, that we might receive the promise of the Spirit through faith" (Gal 3:13-14).

Sadly, some missionaries have purposely ignored doctrines like definite atonement, choosing rather to emphasize the imitating of good behavior as the method of salvation. Others would sometimes boast that they have "no creed but Christ." Instead of preaching about the necessity of the atonement, they try to get people to dress a particular way, talk a

---

1. Matthew 11:29, 2 Corinthians 8:9, 2 Peter 2:21, Ephesians 5:25, and Hebrews 5:8 are all examples of Christ that we must follow.

certain way, and even sing the "right" songs. But without the Gospel and the atonement being the center, these attempts would always prove futile. These churches would become weak, and worship would become weaker.

In summary, those who reject the necessity of the atonement, choosing to preach that we must imitate Christ's moral examples, and those who believe these lies, are still in their sins. We need to get the full Gospel of the cross to them.

- Error: The atonement was good, but it needs to be repeated.

One of the worst attacks against the atonement comes from the Roman Catholic Church. They teach that Jesus' atonement for sins on the cross was not sufficient by itself to save us. Roman Catholics teach that Jesus needs to be regularly, even daily, sacrificed in the Mass. The Reformers rightly called it an abominable practice. Jesus had to be sacrificed once and only once. It is plain wickedness to try to say that he needs to be sacrificed every day. This is one of the more easily refuted errors.

- Hebrews 10:10, "By that will we have been sanctified through the offering of the body of Jesus Christ once for all."
- 1 Peter 3:18, "For Christ also suffered once for sins, the just for the unjust, that He might bring us to God, being put to death in the flesh but made alive by the Spirit."
- Romans 6:10, "For the death that He died, He died to sin once for all; but the life that He lives, He lives to God."
- Hebrews 7:27, "who does not need daily, as those high priests, to offer up sacrifices, first for His own sins and then for the people's, for this He did once for all when He offered up Himself."

The thought that Jesus needs to be sacrificed every day is abominable because it attacks the glorious sufficiency of his work of atonement.

We must therefore avoid situations where we lend credibility to such wicked acts. It is one reason that Christians avoid the Roman Catholic mass.

- Error: God loves everyone in the world, and so Jesus died for them all.

Those who argue that Jesus died for everyone (mis)use the most famous verse in the Bible, John 3:16, and the verses that follow. Here is what John wrote:

> For God so loved the world that He gave His only begotten Son, that whoever believes in Him should not perish but have everlasting life. For God did not send His Son into the world to condemn the world, but that the world through Him might be saved. He who believes in Him is not condemned; but he who does not believe is condemned already, because he has not believed in the name of the only begotten Son of God (John 3:16-18).

One of the principles in understanding the true meaning of a passage in the Bible is to look at the context of the passage. **Doctrines must never be developed based on an isolated verse.**

When did Jesus make this profound statement? Jesus was addressing Nicodemus, a leader of the Jewish people, who came to Jesus in secret. Nicodemus assumed that the Jews were the chosen people of God by virtue of their nationality, and by the covenant sign of circumcision.

So, what was Jesus's message to him? First, Jesus told him that salvation was not a Jewish right by virtue of their nationality or circumcision. Second, Jesus told him that God loves the world, not just Israel. Third, Jesus told him that anyone who wanted to be part of his kingdom had to be born again, whether Jew or Gentile. Fourth, to further add weight to these points, Jesus pointed out that the Jews who did not believe in Jesus were already under condemnation.

Today we can understand this as a warning to those who think they are saved by virtue of their baptism and church membership. Do you see how the context clears our misunderstanding about universal salvation? These verses were to teach the Jews that the new covenant includes Gentiles, like 1 John 2:2—"He Himself is the propitiation for our sins, and not for ours only but also for the whole world."

Consistent with the teaching of Jesus, the Apostle Paul taught that **Jews were not part of true Israel by virtue of their nationality or circumcision but by faith in Jesus alone**. It seems that some Jews were hoping for salvation based on their nationality and circumcision. They made the same mistake as Nicodemus did. Paul clarified this by saying, "But it is not that the word of God has taken no effect. For they are not all Israel who are of Israel" (Rom 9:6).

Yes, Ishmael and Esau were part of Abraham ethnically and biologically, but not part of Abraham's spiritual family by faith. Faith in God's promises alone makes one a child of this redeemed family.

Consistent with the teaching of Jesus, God had long before promised to Abraham the conversion of the nations. He spoke in Genesis 17:4-5, saying "as for Me, behold, My covenant is with you, and you shall be a father of many nations. No longer shall your name be called Abram, but your name shall be Abraham; for I have made you a father of many nations." Later, God promised Abraham that "in your seed all the nations of the earth shall be blessed, because you have obeyed My voice" (Gen 22:18).

Also consistent with the teaching of Jesus, God had promised the conversion of the nations through King David. Look at a Psalm dealing with Christ's suffering to save the world: "All the ends of the world shall remember and turn to the LORD, and all the families of the nations shall worship before You" (Psa 22:27). The promise was passed to King Solomon, consistent with the teaching of Jesus. God promised the conversion of the nations once again, saying "yes, all kings shall fall down before Him; all nations shall serve Him. For He will deliver the needy when he cries, the poor also, and him who has no helper" (Psa 72:11-12).

And consistent with the teaching of Jesus, God had promised the conversion of the nations to the prophet Isaiah through the Suffering Servant described in Isaiah 53, as we saw earlier.

Consistent with the teaching of all the previous writings and Jesus, God had promised the conversion of the nations through the prophet Zechariah, one of the last prophets of the Old Testament; in Zechariah 9:9-10 he said:

Rejoice greatly, O daughter of Zion! Shout, O daughter of
Jerusalem! Behold, your King is coming to you; He is just
and having salvation, lowly and riding on a donkey, a colt,
the foal of a donkey . . . He shall speak peace to the
nations; His dominion shall be from sea to sea, and from
the river to the ends of the earth.

So, why have we looked at all these proofs that God would save
the nations? This makes the point that when Jesus says that God loves
the world, he did not mean every single person in the world, but that he
loved **his sheep <u>from</u>** every nation in the world.

**Further, we find a purpose in Christ's death—indeed a
defined purpose for the elect, that we live no longer for ourselves
but for him**. Paul said "the love of Christ compels us, because we judge
thus: that if One died for all, then all died; and He died for all, that those
who live should live no longer for themselves, but for Him who died for
them and rose again" (2 Cor 5:14-15). His death for us leads to the new
life lived for him.

**If Jesus Christ really died for every single person in the
world and atoned for everyone's sins, then all would be saved and
all would live for him**. Jesus's death could never be a failure.

Furthermore, if Jesus did indeed die for every single person in the
world, God would be unjust. It would have meant that he died for people
who would not be saved, which would open God to the charge of double
punishment.

Further still, the Apostle Paul used the word "all" in 2
Corinthians 5:15 to mean "all kinds," not "every single one." Though
"all" could be translated "every single one," based on what we have seen
above, it would be impossible to interpret that to mean "every single
one." Everyone will not be saved. And surely Jesus did not die in vain.

"All" doesn't always mean "every one," but sometimes means "all
kinds" like in 1 Timothy 6:10—"**the love of money is a root of all
kinds of evil**, for which some have strayed from the faith in their
greediness, and pierced themselves through with many sorrows."

If you looked at the original Greek Paul wrote, you would notice
the words "kinds of" are not there. When scholars were translating the

passage, they put "kinds of" in the text to make Paul's meaning clear to English speakers. So here is the question: Is money the root of all evil? The answer is obvious. No, money is the root of all "kinds" of evil. "All" does not always mean "all" in the universal sense.

Look at some other passages that show that God does not love every single person; there are some people that God definitively hates.

- Psalm 5:5, "The boastful shall not stand in Your sight; You hate all workers of iniquity."
- Romans 9:13, "Jacob I have loved, but Esau I have hated."
- Malachi 1:3, "Esau I have hated, and laid waste his mountains and his heritage for the jackals of the wilderness."

So, we can therefore say that Jesus did not atone for the sins of everyone in the world. That would contradict his word and his nature. Jesus died for his own people.

- Error: Christ made salvation possible to every person in the world.

Some people argue that Jesus did not die for a definite number, but that he died simply to make salvation possible for the world. In their minds, God is at the mercy of the individual's choices, and his hands are tied. Those who teach this error weaken the wonder of Christ's atonement. In reality they are teaching that a certain amount of Christ's atonement will be wasted since all will not accept it. **With a weakened view of the atonement, the greatness of Christ's salvation is minimized**. When salvation is minimized, the wonder of worship is diminished. When the wonder of worship is diminished, Christ is robbed. Will God bless a man who robs him of Christ's glory? On the other hand, when we recognize the greatness of the atonement he made for us, we will see how special our salvation is. And when we see how special our salvation is, our worship will be more passionate.

Arminians who argue that Christ only made salvation possible teach that Christ's atonement simply removed the hurdle of man being able to believe. They treat salvation in two parts: the acquisition of salvation (what Christ purchased for all), and the application of salvation (what individuals choose to do). They emphasize the dual labor in salvation. This is why they argue that man is totally free to make the choice of whether to accept salvation or not. (Total depravity/inability says that man can't make any good choices.) But Christ did not simply remove the hurdle to salvation and make salvation possible. **<u>Christ, our covenant keeper, fully earned salvation by meeting God's full demands of the law for his people</u>**. He did what the first Adam did not do.[2] And then Christ applied salvation by his Holy Spirit to mankind. He moved man to receive Christ's work. So, there is absolutely no room in Christianity for dual labor in salvation, as Arminians believe and teach. God did not simply talk about love and wait to see if man would reciprocate. Man could not reciprocate. God's love drew man to him.[3] You will see more of this in the next chapter.

Furthermore, if we were Arminians, we could believe it possible that Christ could have died and none would be saved, if none chose Christ! How abominable! Arminius was minimizing the work of God and made Christ's atonement seem less rich and less needful. As you can see, the Reformed doctrine of atonement gives glory where it properly belongs—to our loving Savior.

Arminians think their ability to believe and be saved comes from within a man. They think man is capable, without the help of God, to make the choice to believe. By believing this they reject the biblical doctrine of total inability, for no one "seeks after God" (Rom 3:11). Arminians believe that men are sick in sin. But the Bible teaches that men are not sick in sin; men are dead in trespasses and sins, as Ephesians 2:1 and 2:5 teach.

- Error: Definite Atonement limits preaching.

Does the fact of definite atonement—that Christ died for a certain number of people, and every one of them will be saved—limit the preaching of the Gospel? Would definite atonement cause people to become lazy and complacent? This was one of the charges Arminians raised against the Reformed doctrines.

---

2. "For as in Adam all die, even so in Christ all shall be made alive" (1 Cor 15:22).

3. John 6:44.

First of all, if God teaches a doctrine, we must believe it. And God does teach this definite atonement in his Word.

Second, when we make excuses for not doing our assigned work, we must not blame the one who assigns the work. If we shirk our duty, we must never blame God.

Third, let the Scriptures speak! Look at what Jesus said just before he gave the most famous verse in the Bible in John 3:16—"And as Moses lifted up the serpent in the wilderness, even so must the Son of Man be lifted up, that whoever believes in Him should not perish but have eternal life" (John 3:14-15).

Jesus made it clear that Christians must let the world know about what he has done so men might believe in him. That is what we must do. No man knows who the elect are, and no man knows who might believe. **Someone we think might be close to the kingdom might never believe, and the one we think might never believe because his heart seems so cold and hard, might believe and be a great Christian.** We must guard against personal prejudices and laziness. Let the preacher go into all the world and say that Jesus died on the cross for the sins of the world. We do not know exactly who the elect are, but we know God's elect are everywhere. Hear now some of those verses calling us to take the message of the cross everywhere.

- Mark 16:15, "And He said to them, 'Go into all the world and preach the Gospel to every creature.'"
- Matthew 28:19, "Go therefore and make disciples of all the nations, baptizing them in the name of the Father and of the Son and of the Holy Spirit."
- Psalm 22:27, "All the ends of the world shall remember and turn to the LORD, and all the families of the nations shall worship before You."
- Romans 10:14, "How then shall they call on Him in whom they have not believed? And how shall they believe in Him of whom they have not heard? And how shall they hear without a preacher?"

- Acts 1:8, "But you shall receive power when the Holy Spirit has come upon you; and you shall be witnesses to Me in Jerusalem, and in all Judea and Samaria, and to the end of the earth."

Yes, God works his secret purposes of election through the publicly proclaimed Word of God. And the atonement is central in the preaching of God's Word. The preacher's feet, traveling to announce the Good News, were described as beautiful things in Isaiah 52:7! "How beautiful upon the mountains are the feet of him who brings good news, who proclaims peace, who brings glad tidings of good things."

God had one Son, and he sent him as a missionary to preach. He was even called the "Word of God." (John 1:1ff.). We must continue in his footsteps. How will the world hear unless we take this message everywhere or send those who will take it everywhere? Let us send missionaries with our prayers, our money, and our encouragement. It is God's pleasure that men preach the Gospel everywhere.

The Atonement is Our Sure Salvation

Our election is remarkable because a great and holy God cared for meager and sinful us. Remember the background: God made man perfect but man willfully fell into transgression. Instead of loving God and neighbor, Adam hated God and his neighbor, and loved himself. Through Adam we then earned a difficult life on earth, and hell after death for breaking God's law. This punishment is inescapable, unless someone better and perfectly holy took our punishment for us. That one who could take our punishment would atone for our sins! That one was Jesus. And more, because he was also divine, he was great enough to die for the sins of the whole world.

We must never blame God when a man goes to hell. The blame must squarely be placed on man's rejection of Christ's atonement. **Men are not condemned because God didn't elect them. They are condemned because they are in their sin and refuse to look to God for help**. Look at the words of those who murdered Jesus:

Pilate said to them, "What then shall I do with Jesus who is called Christ?" They all said to him, "Let Him be crucified!" Then the governor said, "Why, what evil has He done?" But they cried out all the more, saying, "Let Him be crucified!" When Pilate saw that he could not prevail at all, but rather that a tumult was rising, he took water and washed his hands before the multitude, saying, "I am innocent of the blood of this just Person. You see to it." And all the people answered and said, "His blood be on us and on our children."

Be careful with relationships with Arminians and others who attack or water down the greatness of Christ's atonement. Why? If we married someone who has a weakened view of Christ's atonement, he would not have the same love for God. If he has less love for God, his zeal would be less. If his zeal is less, his worship would be weaker. Would that be good?

<u>Rejoice that the number of those saved by the atonement is so sure that none would be or could be lost.</u> We can rejoice that God does not send all to hell, something all men rightly deserve. The amazing thing is not that God did not choose all, rather, **the amazing thing is that God chose any**. One pastor was heard saying: "Christ did not die for everyone under the sun, but he died for everyone under the Son." Corny? Yes. True? Yes.

Chapter 4

Work of God the Spirit:

Irresistible Grace

Have you ever heard the term "irresistible grace?" "Irresistible grace" is a doctrine that is consistently taught in God's Word. And since this doctrine is taught in the Scriptures, we must make a determined effort to understand it, believe it, and let it affect our lives in such a way that we bring more glory to God. That should be our response to every doctrine. Let's start with defining the term.

Definition of Irresistible Grace

Irresistible grace is God's free, unmerited favor by which he draws unbelievers to become his children, saving them from hell. Without this irresistible grace, people would naturally and willingly walk right into hell.

<u>This grace comes through the Holy Spirit calling the unbeliever by the Gospel of Jesus Christ</u>. The unbeliever surrenders because God's Holy Spirit works in a most effective way, with a sweetness and kindness that only he can do. When God's Holy Spirit works, the unbeliever's questions are answered so that he fully sees his need to surrender himself to God's grace, and he willingly does so.

Other names for this doctrine are "irresistible call," or "effectual call." "Irresistible call" or "effectual call" is the means by which the irresistible grace comes from God. You will see more of this later.

Why Does Man Need Irresistible Grace?

Why doesn't man see his sin by rational and reasonable analysis of the facts, and then surrender to God? That answer, I hope, is apparent now. Man is sinful and in a hardened state of rebellion. He cannot and will not surrender to God, no matter how clearly the case is presented for his sinfulness and guilt.

God must first call us irresistibly, give us grace, and regenerate us. Regeneration is also called being "born again." This is a most appropriate term because it reminds the receiver that his birth was not an act of himself, but the act of another. After all, no one chooses to be born.

The only real Christians are born-again Christians. It is true we live in a society where many people claim to be Christians, but they are Christians in name only, or Christians by tradition. They are still in an unregenerate state. They need the work of the Holy Spirit in their lives.

The Apostle Paul reminded the church in Rome that it is God who must show mercy, as man's will is antagonistic to God's will. **God must call a person in an effectual way**. He said it this way: "So then it is not of him who wills, nor of him who runs, but of God who shows mercy" (Rom 9:16).

God shows mercy by irresistibly calling men and women to himself. He does this knowing that man does not want to come, and neither can he come. The inability of man to come to God is pictured for us in John 3:3-7; there Jesus pointed out to Nicodemus that he had to be born again. The Lord used our natural birth to speak of our spiritual birth. He wanted to point out that we were passive in both. We did not choose to be born; outside forces had to work.

Biblical Proofs of Irresistible Grace

First of all, God uses the Gospel to effectually call the elect to him. There is no mysticism here. There are no dreams. There are no signs in the sky. God uses the Gospel, plain and simple, to call people to himself. Hear the Apostle Paul!

> How then shall they call on Him in whom they have not believed? And how shall they believe in Him of whom they have not heard? And how shall they hear without a preacher? And how shall they preach unless they are sent? As it is written: "How beautiful are the feet of those who preach the Gospel of peace, Who bring glad tidings of good things!" But they have not all obeyed the Gospel. For Isaiah says, "Lord, who has believed our report?" **So then faith comes by hearing, and hearing by the word of God** (Rom 10:14-17).

Earlier in the same letter, Paul had spoken thus: "For I am not ashamed of the Gospel of Christ, for it is the power of God to salvation for everyone who believes, for the Jew first and also for the Greek. For in it the righteousness of God is revealed from faith to faith; as it is written, 'The just shall live by faith' (Rom 1:16-17).

In 2 Corinthians 5:20, Paul directly used the Gospel to plead with the unbeliever to make peace, saying "we are ambassadors for Christ, as though God were pleading through us: we implore you on Christ's behalf, be reconciled to God." In 1 Peter 1:23, the Apostle Peter said the same thing that the Apostle Paul wrote to the church in Rome. He emphasized the working of the Word of God. This is what raised up the spiritually dead—"having been born again, not of corruptible seed but incorruptible, through the word of God which lives and abides forever."

The writer of Hebrews declared that the Word of God exposes our sins and then gives us the salve to heal our wounds: "For the word of God is living and powerful, and sharper than any two-edged sword, piercing even to the division of soul and spirit, and of joints and marrow, and is a discerner of the thoughts and intents of the heart" (Heb 4:12).

When the Word of God works, the new birth takes place. Luke testified to this. He gave an eyewitness testimony in Acts 13:48, saying "when the Gentiles heard this, they were glad and glorified the word of the Lord. And **as many as had been appointed to eternal life believed**."

Second of all, it is when someone hears the Gospel of Jesus that God the Holy Spirit creates faith in his heart. God sends a preacher to the sinner and he preaches of God and his holiness, man and his sin, and Christ and his redemptive work. <u>**The Holy Spirit works that Word in man to create faith in him and pull him to the Savior in an effectual way.**</u> With faith and a renewed will, man then responds and receives the work of Jesus as his own. You see, fundamental to the preaching of the Word is the work of God's Holy Spirit. This is why many who have studied the Bible as simply a historical textbook do not—and cannot—become Christians. **A deaf man may have the best reader reading to him, but he will never hear a voice!** Jesus pointed to the work of the Holy Spirit to draw men to himself, saying in John 6:44, "no one can come to Me unless the Father who sent Me draws him; and I will raise him up at the last day." He also said, "unless one is born of water and the Spirit, he cannot enter the kingdom of God" (John 3:5).

The Apostle Paul spoke of the same thing. And since repetition in the Bible is always deliberate and for emphasis, we must pay closer attention:

- 1 Corinthians 12:3, "Therefore I make known to you that no one speaking by the Spirit of God calls Jesus accursed, and no one can say that Jesus is Lord except by the Holy Spirit."

Look at how closely the Word and the Spirit are linked. The Bible is called the "sword of the Spirit" in Ephesians 6:17—"And take the helmet of salvation, and the sword of the Spirit, which is the word of God."

Look at the work of the Holy Spirit that pulls men to Christ and keeps them there:

- Ezekiel 36:26-27, "I will give you a new heart and put a new spirit within you; I will take the heart of stone out of your flesh and give you a heart of flesh. I will put My Spirit within you and cause you to walk in My statutes, and you will keep My judgments and do them."

We choose Christ, but it is the Spirit who moves us first. He is the first mover in salvation:

- 1 Corinthians 6:9-11, "Do you not know that the unrighteous will not inherit the kingdom of God? Do not be deceived. Neither fornicators, nor idolaters, nor adulterers, nor homosexuals, nor sodomites, nor thieves, nor covetous, nor drunkards, nor revilers, nor extortioners will inherit the kingdom of God. And such were some of you. But **you were washed, but you were sanctified, but you were justified in the name of the Lord Jesus <u>and by the Spirit of our God</u>**."

So, let us warn our Arminian friends against robbing the Holy Spirit of the honor that belongs to him for his work. **It is strange how Arminians talk about gifts of the Spirit and speaking in tongues, and yet they rob him of his rightful honor for our amazing salvation.**

Third, the product of the work of the Holy Spirit through the Gospel is faith. This is a faith for the regenerated to receive the work of Jesus Christ. Without faith we cannot respond.

- Hebrews 11:6, "without faith it is impossible to please Him, for he who comes to God must believe that He is, and that He is a rewarder of those who diligently seek Him."

We would not move a spiritual muscle without faith. We could never do anything to please God. God had to give us everything we needed. We were in worse shape than an unconscious patient in the hospital. We were dead in sin. Seeing our hopeless condition apart from Jesus, do you see how we should love our Savior all the more?

If we go back to the original creation in the Garden of Eden and see how God worked there, we can understand how we are re-created today, how we are regenerated and given faith. At the original creation God made man and gave him everything he needed. Man had nothing by himself. God even had to give him his wife. Man was nothing but dirt. So it is with those who have been saved today! We had nothing and could or would not move by ourselves to get what we needed the most!

Consider Acts 17:28, where Paul said, "in Him we live and move and have our being, as also some of your own poets have said, 'For we are also His offspring.'"

Faith is knowledge of Christ and his work and an ardent trust in the Lord. We have faith to receive what God offers. Simply put, God, and God alone rescued us from darkness and brought us into his Son's kingdom of light (Col 1:13). He then gave us faith, which is like the hand and mouth of the soul, to receive the salvation purchased by Jesus. Faith makes salvation a reality.

Because "we are saved" by God's "grace through faith" which comes from God, and we are "not [saved] by [our] works," we have no ground to boast in ourselves, but in God alone (Eph 2:8-9).

This is the clear teaching of the Apostles, like when Paul said, "you are in Christ Jesus, who became for us wisdom from God—and righteousness and sanctification and redemption— that, as it is written, 'He who glories, let him glory in the LORD'" (1 Cor 1:30-31). This is why God has to destroy our pride first before we can enjoy God's salvation.

Fourth, how do we hear this effectual call to receive this effectual grace? It is not an audio sound like when one hears a preacher. It is an inward call that only those who are aware and alive are able to hear. This is what Jesus taught. Consider the following verses:

- John 10:4-5, "And when he brings out his own sheep, he goes before them; and the sheep follow him, for they know his voice. Yet they will by no means follow a stranger, but will flee from him, for they do not know the voice of strangers."
- John 10:14, "I am the good shepherd; and I know My sheep, and am known by My own."
- John 10:27, "My sheep hear My voice, and I know them, and they follow Me."

The sheep are well aware of their Lord's voice. This is not magic, but a spiritual awakening that God's Holy Spirit works in our lives. Remember, the sheep are spiritually dead before the Shepherd calls them to life. They could not and would not hear his voice.

Once we have received this call, it cannot be undone. If it could be, it would contradict God's character. Paul taught of the irrevocable (permanent) nature of this effectual call, reminding us "the gifts and the calling of God are irrevocable" (Rom 11:29).

When God calls someone, he saves him for life. He does not call and cancel his call. He does not make a mistake like when an umpire makes a call and then cancels it because he made an error, or if he did not see something correctly. When one is born, he is born once and for all. So also, when one is regenerated by the Holy Spirit, he is never regenerated a second time.

In order to justify their position that faith only makes salvation possible, Arminians argue that faith is a common gift—a common type of grace everyone has! They water down faith. They essentially teach that in the true conversion of man no new qualities, powers, or gifts can be infused by God into man's will and therefore, faith is not a gift that God infuses into man. How ignorantly Arminians minimize God's gift! They take a precious gift of faith and attribute it to an "act" of man. They argue that man has a free will and therefore he deserves the credit for faith. Yes, they argue, God gives faith, but it is up to the individual to accept or reject it. To them, faith is like someone offering us zucchinis— if we like them we accept them. If we don't like them we just refuse them. But have we ever seen a dead woman get up and smell the roses on her casket or on her grave? Similarly, we will never see a dead man respond to God's offer of salvation by himself. Faith must be put into us.

What About Irresistible (Effectual) Call and Free Will

Man's free will is only free in theory. Based on what we have seen in the Scriptures, man can only choose to do evil. Man cannot choose to do anything truly good in his unregenerate condition. He will always reject God's offer of mercy because his heart is in rebellion against God. He will always choose what is wrong. So those who argue that man has free will have to understand the limitation of man's free will. And those who argue that man can perfectly choose between right and wrong are denying the full depravity and sinfulness of man.

Because man can only do evil and will always reject every opportunity to put his trust in Jesus, God needs to work effectually to regenerate man's heart so that man might choose him. If God waited for people to make up their minds, none would ever be saved. All would go to hell.

- Philippians 2:13, "for it is God who works in you both to will and to do for His good pleasure."

Someone said it well: "If I had to add one sigh to my salvation, I would be lost forever."

When the Holy Spirit effectually calls, then man responds. He is bound to respond.

What Are the Results of an Irresistible Call

When we are called and regenerated, we repent and change our lives. We hear the Holy Spirit's voice and we are moved to work. He continues to work in us after we are converted. Our life conforms more and more to the image of Jesus Christ. Look at an example of this in Israel's life. God challenged them to respond in faithfulness and choose life. But only those who were regenerated were able to choose obedience. We see this in Deuteronomy 30:15-19,

> **If God waited for people to make up their minds none would ever be saved.**

> See, I have set before you today life and good, death and evil, in that I command you today to love the LORD your God, to walk in His ways, and to keep His commandments, His statutes, and His judgments, that you may live and multiply; and the LORD your God will bless you in the land which you go to possess. But if your heart turns away so that you do not hear, and are drawn away, and worship other gods and serve them, I announce to you today that you shall surely

perish; you shall not prolong your days in the land which
you cross over the Jordan to go in and possess. I call
heaven and earth as witnesses today against you, that I
have set before you life and death, blessing and cursing;
therefore choose life, that both you and your descendants
may live.

When we are called and regenerated, we rejoice in our new life in
Jesus, and we boast about Jesus. We are assured that Christ has called
men into his kingdom by the working of his Holy Spirit. This kills any
personal promotion. There is only ground for praising God. We must
take no credit: "For by grace you have been saved through faith, and that
not of yourselves; it is the gift of God, **not of works**, **lest anyone
should boast**" (Eph 2:8-9). The earliest Church recognized this—"when
they heard these things they became silent; and they glorified God,
saying, 'Then God has also granted to the Gentiles repentance to life'"
(Acts 11:18).

Why Do Some Not Hear This Irresistible Call?

First, some people are not irresistibly called by God. God may
even prevent the Gospel from going to some. After all, election is not a
right! Hell is God's justice. <u>God has no obligation to pull any unbeliever
to himself</u>. Look how the Holy Spirit stopped the Apostles from going
into a certain place to preach the Gospel: "they were forbidden by the
Holy Spirit to preach the word in Asia. After they had come to Mysia,
they tried to go into Bithynia, but the Spirit did not permit them" (Acts
16:6-7).

No one deserves to hear the Gospel. Instead of wondering why
God did not allow some to hear the Gospel, which is his prerogative, we
must be grateful for our Father's election and for the Holy Spirit's
effectual call to us!

Second, people are condemned because they reject the Gospel's
call by the hardness of their hearts. They don't care about God's glory.

They only care about their own pleasures. A man is not condemned because God dislikes him; a man is condemned because of his sinfulness.

Errors Refuted: Irresistible Call

There are some commonly held errors on the doctrine of irresistible/effectual call. While some of these errors have been in the evangelical church for a long time, it is only in the last hundred years or so, with the rise of individualism, that these errors have taken deeper root. It is our duty then to search out the Word of God and expose these errors so that we might rightly give God the glory for his work of redemption.

- Error: Irresistible (Effectual) call can't be true because Jesus couldn't save some that he wanted.

Some Arminians argue that Jesus only made salvation possible, and now his hands are tied. To prove their point, they quote from Matthew 23:37, where it seems to suggest Christ was helpless to save. To the Arminian, Christ's call was a real call, but not an effectual call: "O Jerusalem, Jerusalem, the one who kills the prophets and stones those who are sent to her! How often I wanted to gather your children together, as a hen gathers her chicks under her wings, but you were not willing!" Look at the background of this text before we get the explanation. Jesus has said "woe to you, scribes and Pharisees, hypocrites! For you shut up the kingdom of heaven against men; for you neither go in yourselves, nor do you allow those who are entering to go in" (Matt 23:13).

First, Jesus was referring to the establishment, to the leaders of the Jewish people, who had consistently hindered the Jews from hearing the Gospel. The leaders even threatened to throw those who listened to Jesus out of the synagogues. So, Jesus criticized the leaders for being stumbling blocks to people hearing the Gospel and coming to faith. **Jesus was not saying that his hands were tied and his call**

ineffectual. He was saying that the leaders were hindrances to the Gospel.

Second, the fact that God can effectually move people does not mean he must. **God is not bound to give grace to all, like he is bound to give justice.** He might have been sorry for their condition (in this case, the Jewish condition)—and he was—and yet he chose not to offer them his favor. Some people don't like this teaching because they think all things must be equal, and that all men must have the same help from God, but we must bow to God's revealed will instead of trying to be God. Even in our limited human level we understand that we might choose to help the starving children in Africa rather than Asia, and we would do no wrong in the choice. We are not under obligation to help any, but we graciously help some. Neither is God obligated to irresistibly call anyone!

Third, it was God's deliberate act to leave the wicked in blindness so that they would not believe. Consider Jesus's quoting of Isaiah 6:8 in Matthew 13:14-15—

> And in them the prophecy of Isaiah is fulfilled, which says: 'Hearing you will hear and shall not understand, and seeing you will see and not perceive; for the hearts of this people have grown dull. Their ears are hard of hearing, and their eyes they have closed, lest they should see with their eyes and hear with their ears, lest they should understand with their hearts and turn, so that I should heal them.'

Jesus interpreted these verses exactly as they sound: God would not help some people. As a result, they would remain in their blindness. But was it God who was actively blinding their eyes? No. **Their blindness was from their own sins.** This is very similar language that God used in dealing with Pharaoh prior to the exodus. God is described as hardening Pharaoh's heart, and Moses also wrote that it was Pharaoh who was hardening his heart: "But Pharaoh hardened his heart at this time also; neither would he let the people go" (Ex 8:32); "But the LORD hardened the heart of Pharaoh; and he did not heed them, just as the LORD had spoken to Moses" (9:12).

When God leaves a man without help, man naturally becomes hardened. God is never the source of sin. This is described as God hardening someone's heart.

Many hear the Gospel of Jesus Christ, but to some, the Gospel appears as foolishness because God's Spirit is not working in their hearts. Those who are given the gift of God's Spirit believe the Gospel and are saved. God could save all, but he chooses not to for his own glory. God is exclusionary. That is why there are membership rules in churches. That is why only members of the church are baptized and may participate in the Lord's Supper. God does not treat all men the same way. He is always fair, like when he judges the wicked, but he is also gracious, as when he deals with Christians. We must never attribute evil to the divine persons.

On the other side, there is an erroneous teaching that says: since God calls all his children and none can resist his call, man does not have to make the outward call of preaching the Gospel. They believe Christians do not need to evangelize or send out missionaries to evangelize because the wicked will come if they are chosen. This was one of the arguments raised by Christians in England against sending William Carey as a missionary to India. They were wrong. God inwardly calls the wicked through the outward preaching of the Gospel. We must therefore draw the distinction between the general call (preaching), which the Lord genuinely wants us to make to all men, and the effectual call that the Holy Spirit makes to some who hear the general call.

- Error: The Holy Spirit only irresistibly called those he knew would repent.

In the first case, no man can respond to God unless God's Holy Spirit regenerates him. After all, man is dead and cannot respond to God. So, if the Holy Spirit calls a man irresistibly, it is because he wants that person to respond. In short, the Holy Spirit couldn't look ahead and determine who would repent unless he planned to waken them from their spiritual deadness. That is election, election that is inseparably joined to the irresistible call of God's Holy Spirit. The effectual call is part of that golden, unbreakable chain of salvation. Each part of that chain is inseparably linked to the other parts. This is a relatively easy error to correct for a reasonable mind.

Some Arminians also argue that God calls those who are worthier than others. They think that those who do not get to hear the Gospel are the worst people. That is also easily proved wrong. Israel did not receive salvation privileges because they were better. They were only chosen because God loved them. Election and effectual call are expressions purely of God's love, like we saw in Deuteronomy 7:7, "The LORD did not set His love on you nor choose you because you were more in number than any other people, for you were the least of all peoples."

We were not saved because we were less depraved than others. This is why we ought to love God with a deep passion, and show it by our zealous service.

- Error: The Holy Spirit simply lures people to himself.

Some believe that the Holy Spirit does not irresistibly call men to himself, but instead he lures man like a grandfather may try to bribe a grandchild with candy in order to give her a hug. A grandchild may resist the grandfather, but who is able to resist the effectual call of the Holy Spirit? The ones the Father calls will come!

We may then ask: "What about Acts 7:51, where Stephen said that men resist the Holy Spirit?" Men always resist the Holy Spirit. Man cannot help but fight the Holy Spirit. Acts 7:51 was teaching of the sinfulness inability of man to do good. It was not intended to teach that man is stronger than the Holy Spirit and can resist his effectual call. (Even we who are Christians fight against the Holy Spirit, even years after conversion.) And even though man greatly resists the Holy Spirit, yet, because of the Spirit's power, he is able to give man a new heart to then live in submission to Jesus Christ.

John 6:44 shows that God (through his Holy Spirit) draws men to himself. That word "draw" is not a mild word. It is a word that implies force. **It can be translated "impel" or to "draw by inward power."** In the book of Acts, Christians were drawn or dragged to the authorities as part of the persecution of Christians. The same word is used for fishermen who would drag their nets to catch fish. So, make no mistake about this, this is not God luring, begging, or pleading. This word suggests the almighty power of God at work in man's heart is a power that leads him to surrender. No one can repel the Spirit's call.

If we remember that man is totally unable to do good, it doesn't matter how strong the inducement (lure) to do what is right, man will not do it. He will always choose to stay in his sins.

- Error: The Jews earned salvation by keeping the law and did not need an irresistible call

Some Arminians believe that the Jews moved back to God after the fall by keeping the law. They believe that the Jews were able to do this because man's will did not become "evil" at the fall, but was only somewhat disabled. Furthermore, they believe that God would not have written down the 10 commandments and given them to Moses without man having the ability to keep them. But was that how the Apostle Paul saw the law? No! **If one tried to get salvation by law-keeping he would end up, not in salvation, but in death**.

Because Arminians believe this, they are often legalistic instead of being Christ-centered. They might say to new converts: "You must dress this way, you must act this way in worship, etc." But according to Paul, the law did not encourage man to go to God and obey him. Instead, the law encouraged and aroused man to pursue his own sinful desires leading to death. How does the law arouse man to do contrary to what it says? Man is diametrically opposed to keeping the law. So, when God says, "You shall not steal," the sinner says, "Surely I want to steal." The law only exposes man's sinfulness and condemns him. Paul made this crystal clear, saying

> Is the law sin? Certainly not! On the contrary, I would not have known sin except through the law. For I would not have known covetousness unless the law had said, 'You shall not covet.' But sin, taking opportunity by the commandment, produced in me all manner of evil desire. For apart from the law sin was dead. I was alive once without the law, but when the commandment came, sin revived and I died. And the commandment, which was to bring life, I found to bring death (Rom 7:7-10).

The law in the Garden of Eden was sufficient to bring man the rewards of God, but because of sin, the law lost its effectiveness.

- Error: Man is able to choose God by himself and therefore does not need an irresistible call.

Others argue that man is able to choose God, though it is difficult. In trying to make their point, they (mis)use this passage: "Then Jesus said to His disciples, 'Assuredly, I say to you that it is hard for a rich man to enter the kingdom of heaven. And again I say to you, it is easier for a camel to go through the eye of a needle than for a rich man to enter the kingdom of God'" (Matt 19:23-24). Jesus is not saying that it is difficult to choose God and enter his kingdom; he is saying it is impossible to choose God and enter his kingdom. It is impossible for a camel to go through the eye of a needle. This is a rather poor argument, especially since they conveniently ignore the rest of the story. Let's read it. "When His disciples heard it, they were greatly astonished, saying, 'Who then can be saved?' But Jesus looked at them and said to them, 'With men this is impossible, but with God all things are possible'" (Matt 19:25-26).

Jesus was pointing out that no one can believe unless God makes it possible. Men, by their own actions, cannot be saved. When God works, and only when God works, men can be saved.

We have already looked at many clear passages that prove that God must first effectually call us before we respond and believe. We must use these clear passages to interpret unclear passage like Matthew 19:23-24.

- Error: The Holy Spirit is not making a genuine call if no one can respond.

The Holy Spirit does make a serious and real call to the world, a genuine call. Look at this proof of his genuine call to the world.

- Ezekiel 33:11, "Say to them: 'As I live,' says the Lord GOD, 'I have no pleasure in the death of the wicked, but that the wicked turn from his way and live. Turn, turn from your evil ways!"

Does this look like an insincere call? No, not at all! Look at another example from Isaiah how the Lord called to the world to come and receive the atonement of Jesus Christ.

- Isaiah 55:1-3, "Ho! Everyone who thirsts, Come to the waters; And you who have no money, Come, buy and eat. Yes, come, buy wine and milk Without money and without price. Incline your ear, and come to Me. Hear, and your soul shall live; And I will make an everlasting covenant with you."

But while the Holy Spirit's call is genuine, his call is only effectual to those whom God helps. It is not the fault of the Holy Spirit that man does not hear and respond to his call to repentance. It is not the fault of the Holy Spirit that he does not effectually call everyone who hears the genuine call. **We must not confuse "genuine" call with "effectual" call. They are not the same thing.** All calls to repent from the Holy Spirit are genuine, but not all calls from him are effectual. Because the Lord was pleased to effectually call us, we must be grateful even more for our salvation.

As a result of the rejection of the Holy Spirit's genuine call to the unbeliever, God will condemn him even further. God will ask: "You heard my call, so why didn't you respond?" Man will only be able to say: I did not respond because I was rebellious."

We must preach repentance to all men and wait for God to save those whom he gives the ability to repent. God's Holy Spirit blows wherever he wishes to blow. He regenerates whomever he wishes.

The Effectual Call Leads to Gratitude

We who understand the wickedness of our condition and our total inability to please God would surely understand and appreciate the power of God's effectual grace and call. This will certainly help us to want to serve God better and this will surely humble us.

If I slip and fall on ice, and someone helps me up, I am thankful. If I fall through and am under the ice, into freezing water, with a strong current and someone risks his life to rescue me, which one of the two would I love more? Obviously, I would love the one who did more for me. And that is precisely what we must do, knowing what God has done for us. We must love God better and stronger.

Chapter 5

God Secures His People:

Preservation of the Saints

We now come to the final of what are called the five doctrines of grace. We will learn how God preserves his children and gives them assurance of his grace. And how wonderful it is that God will never save his children and then abandon them.

Definition of the Preservation of the Saints

Paraphrasing a quote I heard some years ago, **preservation is the continuous work of the Holy Spirit in the believer, such that the work of grace that began in the regenerate heart continues to full completion at glorification.**

Historically, some have preferred to call this doctrine "perseverance of the saints." To do so is appropriate as long as we understand that "perseverance" is a gift of God. Through perseverance Christians are preserved. But we prefer to use the term "preservation of the saints" as it prevents others from thinking that human effort is the means by which we are preserved.

Scriptural Proof of the Preservation of the Saints

The "preservation of the saints" was taught in the Old and New Testaments. Our first example is found in Job, which is probably the first written book of the Bible. Job knew, even as he faced death, that only his body would die. God would preserve his soul. He had a stunning assurance of salvation, an assurance that no one could take away from him. He had this assurance because he had faith in his Redeemer. Look at Job's words: "For I know that my Redeemer lives, and He shall stand at last on the earth; and after my skin is destroyed, this I know, that in my flesh I shall see God, whom I shall see for myself, and my eyes shall behold, and not another. How my heart yearns within me! (Job 19:25-27).

Because he had faith in the coming Savior, the Psalmist also had assurance of salvation, long before Jesus was born. He knew God would establish him on solid rock. Jesus is rightly called the Rock of God, like in Psalm 40:2, "He also brought me up out of a horrible pit, out of the miry clay, and set my feet upon a rock, and established my steps."

Let's now look at some New Testament teaching on the preservation of the saints. Jesus indicated that he would preserve his sheep. He secured them in his and his Father's hand, and his Holy Spirit testified to this preservation in our hearts.

- John 10:28-29, "And I give them eternal life, and they shall never perish; neither shall anyone snatch them out of My hand. My Father, who has given them to Me, is greater than all; and no one is able to snatch them out of My Father's hand."

- 1 John 4:13-16, "By this we know that we abide in Him, and He in us, because He has given us of His Spirit. And we have seen and testify that the Father has sent the Son as Savior of the world. Whoever confesses that Jesus is the Son of God, God abides in him, and he in God. And we have known and believed the love that God has for us. God is love, and he who abides in love abides in God, and God in him.

Later in the New Testament, Paul testified that we can know in our hearts that we are always God's children. He was confident that we would be glorified in heaven after death, as you can see in the following verses.

- Romans 8:16-17, "The Spirit Himself bears witness with our spirit that we are children of God, and if children, then heirs— heirs of God and joint heirs with Christ, if indeed we suffer with Him, that we may also be glorified together."
- 1 Corinthians 1:8, "[He] will also confirm you to the end, that you may be blameless in the day of our Lord Jesus Christ.

Paul stated the same fact in a different way: God assures us that we will be saved from judgment, saying in Romans 5:8-9, "But God demonstrates His own love toward us, in that while we were still sinners, Christ died for us. Much more then, having now been justified by His blood, we shall be saved from wrath through Him."

Peter echoed the Lord Jesus, that the Lord will keep his children's souls for eternity, saying "Blessed be the God and Father of our Lord Jesus Christ, who according to His abundant mercy has begotten us again to a living hope through the resurrection of Jesus Christ from the dead, to an inheritance incorruptible and undefiled and that does not fade away, reserved in heaven for you, who are kept by the power of God through faith for salvation ready to be revealed in the last time" (1 Pet 1:3-5).

How Does the Believer Become Assured of His Salvation?

Though we are miraculously saved by God, sin yet remains in us. We sin in thoughts, words and actions. We never stop sinning, even though we are in God's kingdom. We stumble.[1] We know the wicked one never leaves us alone. We need help from God to overcome sin. We will only be perfect in glory. **So Jesus promised to preserve our souls, which he confirmed by praying for our souls**. He also said "this is the will of the Father who sent Me, that of all He has given Me I should lose

---

1. James 3:2; Romans 7:22.

nothing, but should raise it up at the last day" (John 6:39). He personally assured Peter, saying "Simon, Simon! Indeed, Satan has asked for you, that he may sift you as wheat. But I have prayed for you, that your faith should not fail; and when you have returned to Me, strengthen your brethren" (Luke 22:31).

How then does this assurance that Jesus promised come to us?

- **We listen to and believe the Word of God.**

This is the first means of grace. Consider what Paul wrote: "So then faith comes by hearing, and hearing by the word of God" (Rom 10:17). Through listening to preaching, God gives us what we need to grow in grace and to have the strength to thrive. Doesn't a mother give her baby the right food when he is born? Also, you may have seen the famous ad of the lady saying, "I've fallen, and I can't get up." Yet we are equipped with what we need to get up when we fall, and to make it all the way to the end of our lives. God feeds us with good things. Our spiritual bones are strong.

This means we must study the law, prophets, Psalms, Gospels, and Epistles. We must stay away from churches that focus on the New Testament only, or our souls will only get partial nourishment. We must teach these books to our children. Don't use the Bible as a quick snack. Make it the full meal. Study it privately. Paul told Timothy to "Preach the word! Be ready in season and out of season. Convince, rebuke, exhort, with all longsuffering and teaching" (2 Tim 4:2). The Psalmist cried out "Oh, how I love Your law! It is my meditation all the day" (Psa 119:97).

- **We make use of the sacraments.**

The Lord's Supper and baptism are the sacraments of the true Church Jesus founded. The Lord's Supper feeds our soul in a visible way with the work of Jesus on the cross. When our minds focus on the cross it becomes visual preaching, a means of grace. We are reminded of our blessed salvation. Baptism draws our minds to the blood of Jesus that washed away all our sins. That message then sinks into our hearts and we are spiritually nourished.

The Church is the city of refuge where we are fed the Word and sacraments as we wait for our final redemption. But the Word and Sacraments don't work by themselves.

- **We make use of the Word and Sacraments through the Holy Spirit to increase our faith.**

Paul wrote,

> As many as are led by the Spirit of God, these are sons of
> God. For you did not receive the spirit of bondage again
> to fear, but you received the Spirit of adoption by whom
> we cry out, "Abba, Father." The Spirit Himself bears
> witness with our spirit that we are children of God, and if
> children, then heirs—heirs of God and joint heirs with
> Christ, if indeed we suffer with Him, that we may also be
> glorified together (Rom 8:14-17).

You see, when the Holy Spirit works in us, we call God, "Daddy." An adopted child may take a while, but he soon adapts to his new parents. The more we know our Father, the more we trust him. He convinces us that we are heirs of God and joint heirs with Jesus. (Do you see why the minister prays before he preaches and does the sacraments? He wants that Word and sacrament to work assurance in us.)

Look for a moment at some of the spiritual gifts the Holy Spirit gives. These gifts remind us that we were sealed forever by the Holy Spirit and that we must use our gifts for the increasing of the faith of our brothers and sisters.

- Ephesians 4:12-15 "for the equipping of the saints for the work of ministry, for the edifying of the body of Christ, till we all come to the unity of the faith and of the knowledge of the Son of God, to a perfect man, to the measure of the stature of the fullness of Christ; that we should no longer be children, tossed to and fro and carried about with every wind of doctrine, by the trickery of men, in the cunning craftiness of deceitful plotting, but, speaking the truth in love, may grow up in all things into Him who is the head—Christ."

- **We make use of our strengthened faith to worship Jesus.**
This goes without saying. Who could recognize the Lord's wonderful protection and not pour out his heart in worship?

- **We make use of our strengthened faith to work for Jesus.**
**The stronger our faith, the stronger will be our assurance, and the
easier it will be to work for Jesus.** One of our works that shows that
we have the assurance of salvation is fighting sin in the world, the devil,
and our own flesh. This work will not be in vain. Peter recognized this
when he exhorted us, "Be sober, be vigilant; because your adversary the
devil walks about like a roaring lion, seeking whom he may devour. Resist
him, steadfast in the faith, knowing that the same sufferings are
experienced by your brotherhood in the world" (1 Pet 5:8-9). Paul also
pressed us to "not be conformed to this world, but be transformed by
the renewing of your mind, that you may prove what is that good and
acceptable and perfect will of God" (Rom 12:2). He also said "not that I
have already attained, or am already perfected; but I press on, that I may
lay hold of that for which Christ Jesus has also laid hold of me" (Phil
3:12).

We put to death our sin. We practice obedience, replacing sin
with service to a holy God. Instead of wasting time on the internet, we
write an encouraging e-mail to a visitor to church, we say a prayer for the
persecuted or the poor, or we write a letter of encouragement to a
missionary. Let us be willing to drop some of the lesser activities so we
can focus on our souls. This is how we kill lusts!

How We Know We Are Preserved

There is no question that we can assuredly know in our hearts
that we are preserved forever by Jesus. Hear the Apostle John's words:
"These things I have written to you who believe in the name of the Son
of God, **that you may know that you have eternal life,** and that you
may continue to believe in the name of the Son of God" (1 John 5:13);
and "Behold what manner of love the Father has bestowed on us, that
we should be called children of God! Therefore the world does not know
us, because it did not know Him. Beloved, now we are children of God;
and it has not yet been revealed what we shall be, but we know that when

He is revealed, we shall be like Him, for we shall see Him as He is" (1 John 3:1-2).

Paul also confirmed that we can have assurance in our hearts. He is sure of this: "For this reason I also suffer these things; nevertheless I am not ashamed, **for I know whom I have believed and am persuaded that He is able to keep what I have committed to Him until that Day**" (2 Tim 1:12).

What About Backsliders?

Backsliders are true believers who fall away from faithfully serving the Lord for various amounts of time. They may fall so far that it may appear as if they were not believers at all. But backsliders will always return.

How can we be sure that backsliders will always return to the Lord? We can confidently say that because only Christians, those who have eternal life, can backslide. Those who are not Christians cannot backslide because they never left the world. How can they go back from where they never left?

So-called "backsliders" who never return to Christ show that they were never truly believers in the first place! Maybe they were emotionally attached to the church, but they were never part of the true church. John said about them "they went out from us, but they were not of us; for if they had been of us, they would have continued with us; but they went out that they might be made manifest, that none of them were of us" (1 John 2:19).

The one who backslides shows it. The sin in the heart comes out. He will not sing like we ought to sing and be as friendly as we ought to. He won't look forward to celebrating the Lord's Supper. He may even deny knowing the Lord. He might stay in that backslidden state for a long time.

Why do we backslide? Christians backslide because we are drawn away by the lusts of the flesh, the lusts of the eyes, and the pride of life. We backslide because we haven't mortified the lusts of our hearts.

God Secures His People: Preservation of the Saints

How do backsliders come back? God intervenes and brings them back to himself. God knows the backslider cannot get back to him by his own action. **God will send him a message through his Word, like when he called King David after he stole Bathsheba, committing adultery, killing her husband, and then living in a backslidden state for some time.** Look at how God confronted David!

> Then Nathan said to David, "You are the man! Thus says
> the LORD God of Israel: 'I anointed you king over Israel,
> and I delivered you from the hand of Saul. I gave you
> your master's house and your master's wives into your
> keeping, and gave you the house of Israel and Judah. And
> if that had been too little, I also would have given you
> much more! Why have you despised the commandment
> of the LORD, to do evil in His sight? You have killed
> Uriah the Hittite with the sword; you have taken his wife
> to be your wife, and have killed him with the sword of the
> people of Ammon (2 Sam 12:7-9).

And look at the result of the confrontation. David said "I acknowledged my sin to You, And my iniquity I have not hidden. I said, 'I will confess my transgressions to the LORD,' And You forgave the iniquity of my sin" (Psa 32:5). He prayed, "make me hear joy and gladness, That the bones You have broken may rejoice. Hide Your face from my sins, And blot out all my iniquities. Create in me a clean heart, O God, And renew a steadfast spirit within me" (Psa 51:8-10).

David's son, King Solomon, also backslid, and even longer than David did. Solomon abandoned God for many of the middle years of his life. For years he tried pleasures, power, building projects, and many other things to satisfy his soul apart from God. Later in his life he realized the foolishness of his ways. But he only discovered the foolishness of his ways when he entered into God's house and heard the preaching of God's Word.[2]

This is why we must never miss the preaching of the Word of God. This is why we must daily have personal and family devotions, even

---

2. See Ecclesiastes 5.

God Secures His People: Preservation of the Saints

though our lives are busy. God's Word helps to prevent backsliding, and God's Word helps to restore the backslider. It is most common that those who are living in a backslidden state are not hearing the Word of God, so their souls go through a drought.

But don't forget that it is **the Holy Spirit who works through the preaching that leads the backslider to repentance.** The Holy Spirit works because Jesus prayed to the Father on behalf of the backslider, like when he prayed in Luke 22:31-32 for Peter to be restored: "Simon, Simon! Indeed, Satan has asked for you, that he may sift you as wheat. But I have prayed for you, that your faith should not fail; and when you have returned to Me, strengthen your brethren." Jesus continues to do the same thing for his people today. Look how Jesus assumed Peter would be restored because he had prayed for him! For this reason, John calls Jesus our Advocate: "My little children, these things I write to you, so that you may not sin. And if anyone sins, we have an Advocate with the Father, Jesus Christ the righteous" (1 John 2:1). Jesus lives forever to be our Advocate in heaven before his Father!

Why would God restore the backslider? Because God loves his children, and he elected and justified them through Jesus. Yes, the golden chain of salvation cannot be broken. Once God has planted that seed, it will become a full-grown tree. The Apostles Paul and John shared this certainty—

- Philippians 1:6, "being confident of this very thing, that **He who has begun a good work in you will complete it** until the day of Jesus Christ."
- 1 John 3:9, "Whoever has been born of God does not sin, **for His seed remains in him**; and he cannot sin, because he has been born of God."

God does not restore the backslider because the backslider is good. The backslider is not good. He does not realize his sin by himself. **God restores the backslider because God is good.**

- Exodus 34:6, "And the LORD passed before him and proclaimed, 'The LORD, the LORD God, merciful and gracious, longsuffering, and abounding in goodness and truth.'"

- Malachi 3:6, "For I am the LORD, I do not change; therefore you are not consumed, O sons of Jacob."

Even Satan acknowledged that God put a hedge of love around Job and he couldn't touch him.

As we conclude our examination of the backslider, remember that while hell is the natural and sure direction of the backslider, it is impossible for the backslider to go to hell! He cannot go to hell because he is God's child, and he has eternal life. **Eternal life cannot cease to be eternal life, or it wasn't eternal life in the first place**. The divine end for God's elect children cannot change. Remember these promises.

- 2 Thessalonians 3:3, "But the Lord is faithful, **who will establish you and guard you** from the evil one."
- Romans 8:29-30, "For whom He foreknew, He also predestined to be conformed to the image of His Son, that He might be the firstborn among many brethren. Moreover whom He predestined, these He also called; whom He called, these He also justified; and whom He justified, these He also glorified."
- Romans 11:29, "For the gifts and the calling of God are irrevocable."

The Holy Spirit will not and cannot remove his seal or invalidate it, no matter how far into sin a man falls.

- Ephesians 1:13, "In Him you also trusted, after you heard the word of truth, the Gospel of your salvation; in whom also, having believed, you were sealed with the Holy Spirit of promise, who is the guarantee of our inheritance until the redemption of the purchased possession."

Yes, we must be ashamed of our backsliding and repent, **but we must rejoice in God's promise to not abandon us in our sin and shame.**

If You Doubt Your Preservation, It Doesn't Mean You Are Not Saved

Christians will always have doubts about their salvation as long as they are in this world. King David doubted his salvation. In Psalm 13, he wondered where God was, as if he lost his union with God, lamenting,

"How long, O LORD? Will You forget me forever? How long will You hide Your face from me? (Psa 13:1).

Asaph, a Psalmist who likely worked in the temple, wrote about stumbling in his faith. The thought that the wicked prospered and were healthy was too much for him. And he wondered about his salvation. He wondered if it were a waste of time to serve God, crying out "But as for me, my feet had almost stumbled; My steps had nearly slipped... Surely I have cleansed my heart in vain, And washed my hands in innocence" (Psa 73:2, 13).

But even though we may doubt, God will not allow us to be destroyed. He keeps us from falling off the cliff. He always stops doubts from destroying us.

Arminians argue that doubting is "praiseworthy," but they argue this for a sinister reason. They use this argument to push people to fear. Instead of preaching the glorious work of Christ for sinners as the true motivation for good works, **they want us to do good works from fear of falling away and losing our salvation.** That is not a good thing they are doing, because doubting is sin, as the author of Hebrews wrote:

> Therefore, brethren, having boldness to enter the Holiest
> by the blood of Jesus, by a new and living way which He
> consecrated for us, through the veil, that is, His flesh, and
> having a High Priest over the house of God, let us draw
> near with a true heart in full assurance of faith, having our
> hearts sprinkled from an evil conscience and our bodies
> washed with pure water (10:19-22).

So, we must not come to God with fear and doubts. We must come to God with confidence and comfort. If we don't always feel the assurance (most people don't from time to time), it doesn't mean that we are not saved. We have to grab hold of the assurance that God makes available to all his children through his Word and sacraments! Look how Paul grabbed hold of this certainty! He said

> I have fought the good fight, I have finished the race, I
> have kept the faith. Finally, there is laid up for me the
> crown of righteousness, which the Lord, the righteous
> Judge, will give to me on that Day, and not to me only but

also to all who have loved His appearing . . . And the
Lord will deliver me from every evil work and preserve
me for His heavenly kingdom (2 Tim 4:7, 8, 18).

Does Paul appear to have any doubt? No. Neither should we. This is the
teaching of God's Word. So we must read God's Love Letter, the Word
of God, and be reminded of his love and promises.

Errors Refuted: Preservation of the Saints

Let us now examine some common errors that are believed and
taught by some regarding the doctrine of the preservation of the saints.
As we do, keep in mind that this doctrine of the preservation of the
saints was common in the Church until the last 200 years. With the rise
of the modern Pentecostal movement and a lack of biblical scholarship,
blessings from the assurance of salvation have been denied to Christians.

- Error: We have evidence of people who were Christians who are
  no longer Christians.

There are some who argue that there are people who were Christians in
the past, had eternal life, and then lost it. Consider one of those passages
that supposedly proves this: "My people are bent on backsliding from
Me. Though they call to the Most High, none at all exalt Him (Hos 11:7).

Notice that Hosea was not writing about an individual's fall into a
backslidden state. He was writing about Israel wandering from the faith.
And we know that **God never abandoned Israel as a people**. In fact,
soon after Hosea, Israel was sold into Assyrian captivity, but God
promised that Israel would be restored. Romans 11 testifies to their
return. We may not take a principle that applies to a nation in general and
apply it to individuals. For example, in the fifth commandment God
promises long life in Canaan for those who obey their parents. So if
someone in Israel died young, may we conclude that he did not honor his
parents? What about those who did not honor their parents but lived
long? The point is that this was a covenantal promise, a promise that
Israel would remain in the land as long as order was maintained.

There is a second consideration as well. Even if Hosea were referring to individuals, we are taught that those who appear to have fallen from grace did not fall from grace at all. Yes, some temporarily fall into sin, like King David did, but they return to God. Remember, those who were part of the Church, left and never returned were never part of the true Church in the first place. Those who have "eternal" life can't lose "eternal" life. By its very definition, eternal life has no end. That is what the Apostle John wrote of so eloquently, again, in 1 John 2:19— "They went out from us, but they were not of us; for if they had been of us, they would have continued with us; but they went out that they might be made manifest, that none of them were of us."

When Arminians argue that the regenerated can become un-regenerated, they are attacking the richness of God's salvation. They become robbers of God's honor. They are literally arguing that eternal life has an end.

Look at another passage Arminians use to suggest a Christian can become un-regenerated:

For it is impossible for those who were once enlightened, and have tasted the heavenly gift, and have become partakers of the Holy Spirit, and have tasted the good word of God and the powers of the age to come, if they fall away, to renew them again to repentance, since they crucify again for themselves the Son of God, and put Him to an open shame (Heb 6:4-6).

First, this passage was not intended to teach that we could lose our salvation as Arminians believe. We can't lose eternal life. The elect can't become "un-elected." We were the Father's gift to the Son before the foundation of the world.

Second, this passage teaches us that **God keeps and prevents us from losing our salvation**. It was really teaching us what God would do for us. Look at the rest of the passage and see the conclusion in verse 9: "But, beloved, we are confident of better things concerning you, yes, things that accompany salvation, though we speak in this manner."

The writer points out that there was no chance of any Christian falling away! He uses a theoretical possibility to emphasize the greatness

God Secures His People: Preservation of the Saints

of our salvation. Note his words, "though we speak in this manner." We all speak like that at times. We might say: "If a man lifts a rock as heavy as a house, it would crush him." We are not saying that a man could lift a house; we are saying that a heavy weight could crush a man. We always have to consider the context when interpreting the Bible.

Third, even if this verse were to be taken literally, the Arminian argument would be illogical. How? The second part of the verse says that it is impossible for the one who has backslidden and lost his salvation to return. But the Arminian says that the backslider who has lost his salvation can return. They can't have it both ways. Either the backslider is certainly lost forever, or this passage is not speaking of losing salvation.

As Reformed believers, we rest in the assurance that the elect can never lose their salvation, though they can fall away from God's favor for a time. Yes, elect believers succumb to very deep sins at times and can suffer serious spiritual pain from them. They may even be away from the Church of God for a long time. But because they are believers, adopted children of God, God will bring them back. What blessed assurance!

- Error: Persevering is not a fruit of election, but a condition that God placed on man.

Arminians believe that in order to be preserved for eternity, God demands we fix the sin that remains in our lives. They like to quote Philippians 2:12, which says "as you have always obeyed, not as in my presence only, but now much more in my absence, work out your own salvation with fear and trembling." But does the Bible here teach that we are to maintain our own salvation by our power? We have already seen that we are totally unable to come to Christ. God must first awaken us by the Holy Spirit, pull us to himself, and apply the atonement to our hearts. Even after we become Christians, we remember that sanctification, the means by which we are cleaned out, is a work of God. It is called a gift. Then consider that it is God who works in us to will and to do good things, as Paul taught. You see, the Arminian is trying to give man the credit for what God gives to him (perseverance in the faith).

> Paul could hardly have been clearer when he wrote
> He who did not spare His own Son, but delivered Him up
> for us all, how shall He not with Him also freely give us

all things? Who shall bring a charge against God's elect? It is God who justifies. Who is he who condemns? It is Christ who died, and furthermore is also risen, who is even at the right hand of God, who also makes intercession for us. Who shall separate us from the love of Christ? Shall tribulation, or distress, or persecution, or famine, or nakedness, or peril, or sword? (Rom 8:32-35).

Arminians ignore the fact that no man has the power to resist the devil. Only God has that power **and he preserves his Church through that power**.

- Error: Assurance of salvation will make people lazy.

Arminians say that the doctrine of the preservation of the saints will make us lazy and careless. They think that the Christian who falls into sin and is restored will think that he can continue to do what is wrong—like the child constantly hitting his brother and saying "I'm sorry," every time with the hope that his parents will accept that he is truly sorry. They believe that a Christian who is saved will say: "If I am going to heaven, why bother to live godly?" But the fact that we are assured of our salvation does not and must not make us boastful!

But Arminians don't understand the powerful work of God, that when God works in the hearts of sinners they will submit to him more and more, and better and better. If we use Christ's assurance of restoration as an excuse to sin, we don't understand what salvation is! On the contrary, the fact that we are assured of our salvation makes us humble, respectful, godly, patient in conflict, prayerful, and steadfast. We are pressed by the Holy Spirit to speak the truth and to have deep joy in the Lord.

If we were careless and did not tighten the lug nuts on our car wheel and our wheel almost fell off, are we likely to neglect it again? Wouldn't we be even more careful the next time—maybe double-checking to make sure we didn't make the same mistake? Or if we shut the car door on our finger, do we usually do it twice? Similarly, the restored child of God who understands his salvation will be even more careful to walk in God's way! Here are some specifics we will see in our lives once we have been assured of our salvation.

God Secures His People: Preservation of the Saints

With assurance of salvation, we will produce works worthy of our new life. Why? Because God saves us to purify our lives, as Paul told Titus, "[He] gave Himself for us, that He might redeem us from every lawless deed and purify for Himself His own special people, zealous for good works" (Tit 2:14).

With assurance of salvation, we will work to purify ourselves of our sins. If you have salvation you will be actively fighting sin. John said "Beloved, now we are children of God; and it has not yet been revealed what we shall be, but we know that when He is revealed, we shall be like Him, for we shall see Him as He is. And **everyone who has this hope in Him purifies himself, just as He is pure**" (1 John 3:2-3).

With assurance of salvation, we will worship! True worship is evidence of true humility. Worship is making ourselves totally under submission to God! The great worship Psalms capture this, like in Psalm 116:12-13—"What shall I render to the LORD For all His benefits toward me? I will take up the cup of salvation, And call upon the name of the LORD." To "take up the cup of salvation" is to give a picture of thanksgiving (worship), like the head of a household did before a meal. "Call on the name of the Lord" means "to worship."

With assurance of salvation, we will guard ourselves and show that we trust in Jesus. If we aren't close to God, when we work hard and get a lot of money we will forget to guard our soul against wealth, and be lured away into sin. With wealth we can feel powerful so we don't love our wives as we ought to, and our marriages end in divorce. With wealth we can choose creature comforts over kingdom work. If we aren't close to God, when we choose a spouse, we won't pray for wisdom to make a good choice. We then marry a woman that doesn't meet God's standards and we end up worshipping her idols! If we aren't close to God we can become followers of wicked friends and find out that they pull us away from worshipping, or they change how we talk, and we stop caring for the fellowship of believers. If we aren't close to God and his Word doesn't resonate in our hearts, and we sit in front of our computer, we are likely to wander into websites that we shouldn't.

- Error: Only in special ways we can know that we are saved.

Arminians argue that no one can have or experience assurance of salvation unless it is revealed to him by special revelation (prophecies, a dream, someone telling them, or opening up their Bibles randomly to a certain passage, etc.). In doing this they mime what the Roman Catholic popes taught. Yet Romanists go one step further. The Council of Trent, a Roman Catholic Council, issued a curse upon anyone who said he could be sure he was saved—even if he had special revelation. (There are many similarities between Roman Catholicism and Arminianism.) But the Holy Spirit works in our hearts through the Word of God to assure us that we are God's children and secured forever.

The Apostles taught that we could have assurance: "These things I have written to you who believe in the name of the Son of God, that you may know that you have eternal life, and that you may continue to believe in the name of the Son of God" (1 John 5:13).

Elected and Preserved

God preserves those whom he elected and called in Jesus Christ, and he gives us the assurance of our preservation. We experience the assurance of our salvation when the Holy Spirit works through the Word in our hearts and gives us faith to rest in God's promises. **Yes, we then use that faith to persevere in the faith. We could not persevere by our own efforts**.

It is true that sometimes we might doubt our salvation and lose the blessings of our assurance, but God will never allow us to be destroyed. Help will always come.

Knowing that God rescues us when we fall into sin—and again, only because of Christ's suffering, doesn't that make us stop flirting with trouble? Doesn't that warn us not to be lazy? Remember, we shouldn't want to burn our hands on the stove a second time.

Doesn't Christ's assurance of our eternal salvation make us love God more, so that we show it? Doesn't Christ's assurance make us cherish the preached Word of God and his holy sacraments? Doesn't Christ's assurance of our eternal salvation comfort us? Shouldn't we feel sad for those who don't understand assurance and so rob themselves of the benefits of it? Won't that motivate us to tell them that they can enjoy the gift of assurance? We are preserved in faith because we are elected from eternity past.

Chapter 6

The Nature and Function of

the Church

The Church is the bride of Christ drawn from every nation under the sun. Revelation 21:9 makes that point clear. Being a bride has its implications. What are the implications of being Christ's bride? If the Church were the bride of Christ, then the Church is under the rule of the Bridegroom and must faithfully perform her duties.

In order for the bride to function properly, the Bridegroom, the Lord Jesus Christ, established different offices with different functions to keep order in the Church, and to help her do her work and live up to the family name. The Bridegroom also teaches the bride her duties. This chapter will focus then on the duties of the Church, the bride of Christ, and how the Church must perform her duties.

Who Runs the Church?

There are three main types of Church government common today. **First, there is the Congregational form of government**. This is when a congregation has no formal or institutional relations with other congregations, and the elders are accountable to no one except the local congregation. (Congregational churches may have a loose or informal affiliation with other churches.) This is common in many Baptist churches. **Second, there is the hierarchical system of government** where the congregation is under the pastor, and he is accountable to an overseer or bishop over him, and so on. Authority is like a pyramid going upward. **Third, there is the Presbyterian system of government** where all pastors, elders and deacons are under the supervision of other pastors, elders, and deacons. No leader in the Church can be a law unto himself; Christ has the ultimate power. The Presbyterian form of government is the government established by the Lord. Most Reformed churches have a Presbyterian system of government.

These rulers of the Church rule under the Good Shepherd, as it is his Church. The Church is visible. Jesus emphasized the presence of the local church.[1] He expects people to be a part of it. There are no secret meetings.

The Church is not a democracy, run according to the dictates of the members or the leaders. Jesus Christ paid for the freedom of the Church and she belongs to him. Only he says how his church is run.

Elders

Who Are They?

Elders are the spiritual overseers of the Church. They ensure that the preaching of the Word of God, the administration of the Sacraments, and Christian discipline are properly done.

Another word for elder in the Greek language, the original language of the New Testament, is the word "presbyter." You notice that we get the word "Presbyterian" from it. A Presbyterian church is a church that is run by the elders. (But do not be confused! A Presbyterian

---

1. When I write Church with a capital "C," it means the Church as a whole, universal body. When church with a lower case "c," it means a local church body.

church may be a good one or a bad one. The name only means that it is ruled by elders.) **A presbyter was simply one who oversaw the spiritual matters of members of a church**. Consider two passages that use the word "presbyter" in Greek, where word is translated "elder" in English.

- Acts 20:17, "From Miletus he sent to Ephesus and called for the elders of the church."

- Titus 1:5, "For this reason I left you in Crete, that you should set in order the things that are lacking, and appoint elders in every city as I commanded you."

Another word for elder is "pastor." Pastor comes from the same root word from which we get the word "pasture." This means that the pastor is one who is taking care of feeding the sheep. This is why this title is especially used for the one who regularly teaches the Word of God.

Another word for elders is "bishop." Bishop, which comes from the Greek word *"episcopos,"* is the proper or official title of the pastor. Though the word bishop sounds very different from episcopos if you simply change the "p" to a "b," as many eastern countries do, you will get the word "e-biscop."

Another word for elder is "overseer." This title describes the work of the elder. He oversees the spiritual activity of a church. Look at how these words are used in relation to each other, proving they refer to the same person.

- Acts 20:17, "From Miletus he sent to Ephesus and called for the elders of the church."

Paul called for the "presbuteros" of the church in Ephesus, a word which is translated "elders."

- Acts 20:28, "Therefore take heed to yourselves and to all the flock, among which the Holy Spirit has made you overseers, to shepherd the church of God which He purchased with His own blood."

As he addressed these presbyters (elders) from Ephesus, he spoke of their work and the nature of their work. They were to be overseers of the flock and to do so with the care of the shepherd (pastor). So, the elders are called to be overseers (episcopos, bishops), and shepherds. All five names (elders, presbyters, bishops, shepherds, pastors) refer to the same person.

We do make a distinction between elders who primarily teach and those who primarily rule. The teaching elders are called "teaching elders" in Presbyterian circles, and they are called ministers or Reverends in the continental Reformed traditions. Some churches may have an elder who is a trained counselor and he is called a counselor.

Elders: What Are Their Qualifications?

The one who desires to serve as an elder is seeking a good position. Paul said "This is a faithful saying: If a man desires the position of a bishop, he desires a good work" (1 Tim 3:1). There must not be any compulsion or pressure to serve. The one who serves must sincerely feel the call of God to serve.

Let us now look at the passage that speaks more explicitly of an elder's qualifications. And remember, God determines what the qualifications are, as it is his Church. Only God has the right of divine appointments. When churches appoint "nice" guys to rule who are not qualified, they are acting contrary to God's law. When churches want to give each one "a turn" without that person being qualified, they are acting contrary to God's law.

The qualifications are as follows:

A bishop then must be blameless, the husband of one wife, temperate, sober-minded, of good behavior, hospitable, able to teach; not given to wine, not violent, not greedy for money, but gentle, not quarrelsome, not covetous; one who rules his own house well, having his children in submission with all reverence (for if a man does not know how to rule his own house, how will he take care of the church of God?); not a novice, lest being puffed up with pride he fall into the same condemnation as the devil (1 Tim 3:2-6).

Elders must be blameless. The Lord was not demanding a perfect man, but one who was not notoriously sinful or scandalous. God demands that elders be blameless. But what does "blameless" mean? "Blameless" in Greek meant "unexceptionable." It means that nothing sinful jumps out when one looks at the life of the one who desires to serve as an elder.

Elders must also be monogamous men. This means he must only have one wife. This characteristic was necessary as one is better equipped to lead, having experience in leadership. In the early Church there were some who had multiple wives before they became Christians. The Apostle Paul did not require that they divorce their wives when they were converted, but he limited their ability to serve in the Church as leaders. Further, this contradicts the Roman Catholic doctrine of the superiority of singularity. Leaders in the Church were expected to be married. Roman Catholics take the Apostle Paul's instruction in the figurative sense and suggest that he meant one had to be married to the Lord. This makes no sense, as the Apostle showed that one had to be married and rule over his household well, keeping his family in submission. He further pointed out that if a man cannot rule his household well he is not fit to rule in the Church.

Historically the need for being single was because of the persecution of Christians by the Romans, not because it was superior to remain single. The temporary encouragement, not requirement, by the Apostle Paul in 1 Corinthians to remain single was to avoid men leaving many widows and orphans after they were martyred.

Elders must be temperate or vigilant men. I prefer the word "vigilant" from the King James Version. It means to be wakeful and watchful, diligent in business, and to have a mind clear of distractions. Elders must be vigilant because wolves bring false doctrines into the Church to destroy it. Peter, an elder as well as being an Apostle, said "be sober, be vigilant; because your adversary the devil walks about like a roaring lion, seeking whom he may devour" (1 Pet 5:8).

Elders must also be sober-minded. This is the figurative sense of "sober"; it does not refer to drinking too much. If an elder were not sober-minded, discipline would surely become corrupted in Christ's Church. The elders would act on impulse rather than by God's direction.

Elders must be well-behaved. They must be beautiful in words and works.

Elders must be hospitable. Literally, the word for hospitality is "a lover of strangers." It is easy to love people you know, but it is not easy to love strangers. Elders must entertain according to their ability, based on true love. There were many Christians in the early Church who were homeless because of persecution. So, there was a great need for hospitality.

Elders must be able to teach. This implies that they must have good communication skills and mental ability. They must have the knowledge to teach, so they must be well trained in the Bible. This knowledge and ability to teach can only be attested to by others. So, an elder may not ordain himself. In Apostle Paul's example of the Ephesian elders in Acts 20, we know that those men were likely trained for three years while Apostle Paul lived there. Some churches say that because the church has a minister who does the teaching, elders only have to rule, but both elders and ministers must be able to teach.

Elders must not be drunkards. Clearly there was no intention of preventing the use of alcohol. The Apostle Paul simply wanted to stop the abuse of it. 1 Corinthians 11 confirms that real wine was used in church services to celebrate the Lord's Supper. The Lord Jesus made and drank wine. But drunken men, especially drunken elders, are a disgrace to the Lord.

Elders must not be violent or a striker. They must be non-violent in their actions and in their words.

Elders must not be greedy. Literally, they must not be "lovers of money." The must not be a lover of money because the "love of money is the root of all kinds of evil" (Tim 6:10).

Elders must be gentle. This is in opposition to the striker with fist and words. Elders must say and do things gently. Elders also must not be quarrelsome. Paul emphasized this in 2 Timothy 2:24, saying "a servant of the Lord must not quarrel but be gentle to all, able to teach, patient."

Elders must not be covetous. Covetousness is bad in anyone, but it is worst in an elder or pastor. Elders are called to give. Covetousness is the mother of all sins.

Elders must rule their houses well, having submissive children. The word for rule is "to preside." Literally, a man is president of his home. Elders must provide for and keep discipline there. They must do this in all reverence or gravity. They must not have their children in subjection with all austerity, but with all gravity and weight. When they are able to do this, they can rule a congregation better.

Elders must not be new Christians, or novices. "Novices" comes from a Greek word meaning "new plant." A novice would be "puffed-up" easily. If elders were new Christians and appointed as elders, they might run the risk of becoming arrogant and autocratic in their dealings with Christ's Church. This was Satan's problem in heaven. Elders must demonstrate Christ and have a good testimony to those inside and outside the Church: "he must have a good testimony among those who are outside, lest he fall into reproach and the snare of the devil" (1 Tim 3:7).

If the elders did not have these characteristics, they would bring shame to the Church and to the Lord who bought her. Elders must always remember they rule under Christ. Elders are not representatives of the people; they are representatives of Jesus.

Peter once more speaks to elders: "Shepherd the flock of God which is among you, serving as overseers, not by compulsion but willingly, not for dishonest gain but eagerly; nor as being lords over those entrusted to you, but being examples to the flock" (1 Pet 5:2-3).

Elders: How Were They Elected?

Elders were ordained by God to rule the Church. Elders appoint other elders. It seems the earliest congregations were asked to approve the call of someone to the office of elder. In another instance we see that the Apostle Paul called on Titus to appoint elders in all the churches. Look again at Titus 1:5: "For this reason I left you in Crete, that you should set in order the things that are lacking, and appoint elders in every city as I commanded you." But we may not draw too much from this as the leaders, like Paul, were Apostles who had the authority to write Scripture. So we may not use whatever the Apostle did and think we may simply copy his actions. We cannot know the mind of a believer, as Peter did when he confronted Ananias. Instead, we must look to make sure that elders meet the qualifications outlined above before they are appointed to this holy office. Further, many understand this to mean that Titus was called to appoint those who were elected by the congregation. This makes sense, particularly in light of what you will see below when deacons were elected.

We will reserve our examination of whether women might be elders to when we study whether women might be deacons, as the principles are virtually the same.

Deacons

Who Are They?

The early church in Jerusalem was expanding rapidly. This was a great blessing. But along with the rapid expansion came a problem. The disciples were busy with teaching while other things were not getting accomplished. The Church was not functioning properly. Foreign born widows in Jerusalem were not cared for as they ought to have been. Local widows were given special favor at the expense of foreign born widows (Acts 6:1). And the elders were too busy with preaching and prayer to be involved with the distribution of food sent by foreign Christians.

Lack of care for foreigners was a thorn in Israel's side in the past, and the elders did not want to see this happen again. God had warned them to care for the widows, orphans, and foreigners. Consider how angry God was about the poor treatment of widows, orphans, and foreigners in the past— "And I will come near you for judgment; I will be a swift witness against sorcerers, against adulterers, against perjurers, against those who exploit wage earners and widows and orphans, and against those who turn away an alien—because they do not fear Me, says the LORD of hosts" (Mal 3:5).

Surely the disciples did not want to be guilty of this. Caring for widows and the poor is a fundamental duty of the Church. This call was sounded again later by James, when he said "Pure and undefiled religion before God and the Father is this: to visit orphans and widows in their trouble, and to keep oneself unspotted from the world" (Jam 1:27).

In order to meet this need, under the inspiration of the Holy Spirit, **the disciples called for some to be appointed to care for those unable to meet their own physical needs**: "then the twelve summoned the multitude of the disciples and said, 'It is not desirable that we should leave the word of God and serve tables. Therefore, brethren, seek out from among you seven men of good reputation, full of the Holy Spirit and wisdom, whom we may appoint over this business'" (Acts 6:2-3).

The word that is translated "leave" in English in verse 2 literally meant "to forsake." **The Apostles did not want to forsake their more important duty so they told the believers to select men whom they could appoint as helpers, or deacons**, to fulfill these duties.

What were some of those duties? Deacons were to receive and distribute donations that were coming from richer congregations to help the poor in Jerusalem. They were to verify that the poor were indeed poor. They had to keep account of the tithes and gifts that were brought to worship. They probably kept records of those who were persecuted or arrested. In short, they did whatever they could to allow the elders to dedicate their time to the teaching of the Word of God and praying for the saints. In addition, today deacon's work might include setting up facilities for worship, clearing snow, paying the church bills, and so forth.

Missionaries in foreign countries need to take note that their primary function is not giving food, or digging of wells for water, but preaching the words of life. **While giving food and digging wells are good things to do, they can distract from the main work of the minister.**

Furthermore, without properly functioning deacons, we would likely end up with bigger civil governments who feed the poor and take care of other physical needs. These bigger governments then overtax the population to help the poor. With less money to give to the Lord's work, we get a weaker church and weaker families. The church community is then no longer dependent on each other.

Deacons: What Are Their Qualifications?

The Lord gave his qualifications for this noble office, which Paul spells out in 1Timothy 3:8-13:

> Likewise deacons must be reverent, not double-tongued, not given to much wine, not greedy for money, holding the mystery of the faith with a pure conscience. But let these also first be tested; then let them serve as deacons, being found blameless. Likewise their wives must be reverent, not slanderers, temperate, faithful in all things. Let deacons be the husbands of one wife, ruling their children and their own houses well. For those who have served well as deacons obtain for themselves a good standing and great boldness in the faith which is in Christ Jesus.

Deacons must be reverent. This means deacons must have a good relationship with the Lord. This will cause them to be careful in their duties.

Deacons must not be double-tongued. This means that deacons must treat each one fairly. They must not be like serpents with forked tongues that say one thing to one person and another thing to another person. They must be known as men of truth.

Deacons must not be drunkards. It is true that God forbids all drunkenness, but deacons must have a very high standard. Those who lose control of their ability to reason cannot be expected to be reasonable in their service. How can deacons be expected to teach others to handle money when they do not have control over more important things, like their own minds?

Deacons must not be greedy for money. If deacons are greedy, how can they give to those in need? Remember that the "love of money is the root of all kinds of evil" (1 Tim 6:10). Since one of the main jobs of the deacons is to collect and distribute money, how can they effectively do this if they are greedy?

Deacons must hold the Gospel with a pure conscience. This consciously and constantly reminds them of the purpose they are serving. They will always remember whose they are: Christ's.

Deacons are to be examined to see if they have these qualifications. This is what is meant by "tested." No one is to be put to this office because he is a "good" man or because he is a "nice" man.

Deacons must be blameless. This flows from the examination of their lives. They must not have any blatant or big sins. No great sin must jump out.

Deacons must have good wives. God gives more details about the wives of deacons than the wives of elders. He knew that deacons' wives often had more and constant interaction with the lives of the members of the local church. Deacons' wives must be blameless like their husbands. Their wives must not be misusers of their tongues, but be self-controlled and faithful in all areas of life.

Deacons cannot be polygamous, having more than one wife.

Deacons must have their children under submission. The man who does not rule his family well is not able to rule the Church of Jesus Christ well. The experience a man has to rule over his wife and children helps to qualify him for this ministry.

The foundation or summary of these qualifications is that these men have a good reputation, are filled with the Holy Spirit, and have wisdom.

How Are Deacons Selected and Ordained?

Based on Acts 6, deacons were chosen by congregations. Seven men were chosen because seven were adequate to meet the needs of the church there.   After they were chosen, the elders appointed those deacons to office. So, this was not a system of giving the office to a buddy or a conspiracy by a few. These men had to reach rigid qualifications. After they were selected the elders laid their hands on them and prayed for them. This laying on of hands showed that they were conferring upon the deacons the authority that the Lord had given to them. It was a simple process of passing on authority. There was no symbolic cross on the chest and there was no burning of incense as some religions or sects do.

Should Women Be Deacons?

There are verses in some translations that suggest that women were deacons in the Church. Some therefore argue for female deacons today. Look at one such verse. The word "servant" can be translated "deacon" in Romans 16:1—"I commend to you Phoebe our sister, **who is a servant** of the church in Cenchrea."

First, **the word "deacon" does not always apply to the special office of deacon**. The Church simply took a general word for servant and used it to designate a spiritual servant position in the Church. Consider how the common word "elder" was given a specific spiritual designation also. An elder is an older person (general sense), but an elder is a bishop, pastor, or overseer (special sense) in the Church. Similarly, servant/deacon, a general word, can also be a specific office. Now prior to the word "deacon" being used as a title, it was used to designate any servant of a king, or to a waiter who served food or drink. That general meaning of "deacon" remained, but a special meaning was assigned to it as well. The context determined the meaning. This is not unique. In many eastern cultures we address an older person as "uncle" or "grandpa" by reason of age, not because he is related to us by blood.

Second, women could not qualify to be deacons in the Church. In the clear words of 1 Timothy 3, we see that one of the qualifications for deacons is that they are able to rule their houses well, having their wives and children in submission. And **since only husbands rule (ruling which helps them to prepare), how could a woman be given an office for which she could not prepare?**

Third, **if a woman were appointed as deacon, it would mean she had authority over her husband,** as deacons do have authority over the congregation. This is explicitly forbidden in 1 Timothy 2:12-14, where Paul teaches, "I do not permit a woman to teach or to have authority over a man, but to be in silence. For Adam was formed first, then Eve. And Adam was not deceived, but the woman being deceived, fell into transgression."

For women to be deacons in the church the whole structure of the family, as ordained by God, would have to be changed.

With all this said, the Lord was not saying that women were not smart enough to do this work. But he simply knew that order was important. He is not a God of confusion. If all are equal in authority then anarchy would result. As the Chinese say: "You can't have two tigers in one mountain."

Fourth, **the office of deacon is explicitly a male-only position.** In 1 Timothy 3:12, there is a word that is very important to examine: the word "husbands." This word is a "sex-specific" word. This means it is never, ever used to refer to a woman. The word "man" can be used to refer to "people," but the word for "husbands" can never be used to refer to women.

It is possible that the wives of deacons were called deaconesses. Though Phoebe was not ordained to the Church to be a deacon in the special sense of the word, she could have been given the title based on the role of her husband.

Classis/Presbytery/Synod

Elders do not rule the Church in isolation. If something were too difficult for them to deal with, or they were unsure of a decision, they would call for elders in neighboring churches for advice. **The formal organizing of these churches for advice is called a "classis" or a "presbytery."** A classis or presbytery is usually in a local geographic area. The classis/presbytery is useful for the members of the congregation as well. For example, if they disagreed with the decision of their local elders, they may appeal the elders' decision to the neighboring churches.

Churches within a classis may work together on projects of common interests, like jointly supporting and overseeing mission works, especially if one congregation were not able to financially support a mission work by itself.

It is possible to appeal the decision of a classis or presbytery, if one disagreed with it, to the national association of churches, sometimes referred to as a "synod" or "general assembly."

These greater church bodies help to prevent totalitarianism or anarchy in local churches, as is possible with both the hierarchical and congregational churches.

The Duties of the Bride

The Centrality of Preaching in the Church

The preaching of the Gospel of Jesus Christ is central to the survival of the Church. The Church that does not put preaching as central will starve and likely die. Hear Paul's warning to Timothy:

> These things I write to you, though I hope to come to you shortly; but if I am delayed, I write so that you may know how you ought to conduct yourself in the house of God, which is the church of the living God, the pillar and ground of the truth. And without controversy great is the mystery of godliness: God was manifested in the flesh, justified in the Spirit, seen by angels, preached among the Gentiles, believed on in the world, received up in glory (1 Tim 3:14-16).

The Church must preach of salvation. The Apostle Paul wanted Timothy to preach of Jesus Christ's immaculate conception and his incarnation, which was a miraculous mystery. Paul exhorted Timothy to preach of the union of Jesus Christ's divine and human natures, to show how Jesus had to be man and die as a man because man sinned. He reminded Timothy to show how Jesus had to be divine in order that he might be able to take the full force of God's wrath. He wanted Timothy to speak of the humiliation of Jesus Christ, specifically, that he had to leave the comforts of heaven to be born, live and die as a man, and to speak of the necessity of Jesus Christ's death in order to satisfy an angry God. Paul wanted Timothy to speak of the resurrection of Jesus Christ, which confirmed every truth he had taught, including our resurrection, to speak of Jesus Christ's ascension into heaven, and his ruling from heaven through the Church. Timothy, like all pastors, was to speak of Jesus Christ's return to gather the living and the dead who believe in him, to speak of Jesus as the only means by which man can be saved from sins, and that God would justify the wicked solely on the merits of Christ's righteousness. This meant that pastors were, and are, to preach the Gospel to whomever will listen, not just to the Jews. Any church that does not preach the full Gospel of Jesus Christ is not a true church of Jesus Christ.

The Bible is sufficient for this work: "All Scripture is given by inspiration of God, and is profitable for doctrine, for reproof, for correction, for instruction in righteousness, that the man of God may be complete, thoroughly equipped for every good work" (2 Tim 3:16-17). The Church must preach what the Scriptures say of sanctification. Timothy had to show how true doctrines lead to personal and practical godliness, godliness so clear that salvation would be beyond dispute or doubt.

The Church must preach about restoring those who have strayed. Preaching brings back the straying. Paul speaks of the various ways people stray, saying in 1 Timothy 4:1-3,

> Now the Spirit expressly says that in latter times some will
> depart from the faith, giving heed to deceiving spirits and
> doctrines of demons, speaking lies in hypocrisy, having
> their own conscience seared with a hot iron, forbidding to
> marry, and commanding to abstain from foods which
> God created to be received with thanksgiving by those
> who believe and know the truth.

The phrase "latter times" means any time after the time of the Apostle Paul's writing. Throughout history we find that many departed from the faith, or more specifically, left the Church. Some of these people left because they were fooled by deceiving men who were preaching the doctrine of demons, as all false religions do.

If this Gospel is not preached, the Church will not be built-up, especially considering the intensity of opposition that is faces. Worse, if the Gospel is not preached, the Church will become infected and those who are already inside will be deceived and be led away into false doctrines.

If the Gospel is preached and believed, blessings will flow to all those who are members of Christ's Church.

Furthermore, the preacher must preach from every part of the Holy Scriptures. The Apostle Paul rightly warned Timothy to preach from all Scriptures, which includes all of the Old Testament, even though those books are often ignored.

Discipline

Elders in Christ's Church exercise discipline in the congregation to make sure members are not straying from covenant faithfulness. Jesus gave them this authority in Matthew 16:19, "And I will give you the keys of the kingdom of heaven, and whatever you bind on earth will be bound in heaven, and whatever you loose on earth will be loosed in heaven."

Discipline is not for personal vendettas. In the past, Roman Catholics punished people because they did not meet the traditions and desires of archbishops, cardinals, and popes. We can see an example of this abuse of discipline in the life of many of the early Reformers. Martin Luther, for instance, was threatened and pushed out of the RCC for advocating for faithful Christian teaching. The Church authorities could not refute Luther's argument so they removed him from service in the Church. Another example of abuse of discipline was when the Roman Catholics burned John Hus at the stake for preaching the full Gospel.

There are other churches that do not practice discipline at all. Some do not even have a membership roll, so they don't know whether someone is a member or not. Others are afraid to exercise discipline because they believe that many people might leave the church. Others refuse to exercise discipline because they are afraid that there might be less tithing. Of course, these are all wrong reasons to avoid discipline.

Discipline is practiced for the correcting of faults. In other words, **discipline is restorative**. The goal is to make and keep the Church holy—clean and pure. When the Church is clean and pure, Christ is glorified. Paul frequently spoke of discipline and its goal:

- 1 Corinthians 5:4-5, "In the name of our Lord Jesus Christ, when you are gathered together, along with my spirit, with the power of our Lord Jesus Christ, deliver such a one to Satan for the destruction of the flesh, that his spirit may be saved in the day of the Lord Jesus."
- Titus 3:10, "Reject a divisive man after the first and second admonition."
- 2 Thessalonians 3:6, "But we command you, brethren, in the name of our Lord Jesus Christ, that you withdraw from every brother who walks disorderly and not according to the tradition which he received from us."

We therefore must not resist the efforts of elders to carry out godly discipline.

The principles of church discipline are outlined in Matthew 18. There is no biblical warrant for shunning, as some denominations do. The child of God is punished with a view that he would be restored. He must never be treated worse than a non-believer. We do not refuse to talk to a non-believer, and neither should we refuse to talk to someone who is under discipline.

Sacraments

Elders must faithfully administer the Lord's Supper and baptism for the spiritual nourishment of the local church. The Church is the only place where the Lord's Supper is served and the only place where believers are baptized. There are no private Lord's Suppers or private baptisms. And since the Church and the sacraments belong to Christ, both must be administered according to the directions of Christ. This is why, for instance, we do not baptize the dead. And only those who are authorized by the local church may administer the sacraments.

Christ instituted two, and only two, sacraments: baptism and the Lord's Supper. Both of these sacraments remind us of the work of Christ for sinners and cause our souls to be nourished. Baptism reminds us that our sins have been washed away by Christ's blood. The Lord's Supper reminds us that Christ's body was broken and his blood was shed for our sins. **When we receive these reminders by faith, our souls are nourished.** The RCC added five more sacraments. Some Charismatics have more than two, though some have abandoned what were once held to be sacraments, like washing of the saints' feet.

Since the Lord's Supper is only for those who submit to Jesus, it should never be given to those who do not show that they are submitting to the Lord. We show our submission by living for Jesus, worshipping our heavenly Father, and being a member of a true church. If we are living in rebellion, we must not participate in the Lord's Supper. Elders have the obligation to prevent, as much as they are able, those who wish to participate in the Lord's Supper in an unworthy manner. **Elders show a lack of care for the souls of men if they allow unworthy people to participate in the Lord's Supper**. Paul made it clear it is no ordinary meal:

> Therefore whoever eats this bread or drinks this cup of
> the Lord in an unworthy manner will be guilty of the body
> and blood of the Lord. But let a man examine himself,
> and so let him eat of the bread and drink of the cup. For
> he who eats and drinks in an unworthy manner eats and
> drinks judgment to himself, not discerning the Lord's
> body (1 Cor 11:27-29).

Baptism is a requirement of every Christian to show that he is trusting in the Savior, and that he knows his sins have been washed away—"Then Paul said, 'John indeed baptized with a baptism of repentance, saying to the people that they should believe on Him who would come after him, that is, on Christ Jesus.' When they heard this, they were baptized in the name of the Lord Jesus" (Acts 19:4-5). Those

who truly believe and are baptized are obligated to have their children
baptized as well. This shows that those children are members of the
covenant. You will see more of this later.

Evangelism

**The Church, Christ's bride, is commanded to evangelize. It
is part of our sanctification process.** The bride who has a new heart is
aware of her previous condition and desperately wants to see those in
that same condition saved. The bride who sees how her record was made
clean will want to tell others how to get their record clean. Paul even calls
us ambassadors: "we are ambassadors for Christ, as though God were
pleading through us: we implore you on Christ's behalf, be reconciled to
God. For He made Him who knew no sin to be sin for us, that we might
become the righteousness of God in Him" (2 Cor 5:20-21).

**The bride who has heard the voice of her Savior will want to
obey that voice to call other sheep into the fold of the Good
Shepherd.** She is called to "enlarge her tents" (Isa 54:2). Jesus left his
Apostles with this very command, saying,

> All authority has been given to Me in heaven and on
> earth. Go therefore and make disciples of all the nations,
> baptizing them in the name of the Father and of the Son
> and of the Holy Spirit, teaching them to observe all things
> that I have commanded you; and lo, I am with you always,
> even to the end of the age (Matt 28:18-20).

How will this be done? The bride of Christ will speak the truth in
love, she will bring the message with zeal, she will mark the message with
the love of Jesus Christ in her life, and she will speak the truth to the
unsaved with boldness. Paul lays these things out in Ephesians 6:18-19:
"[pray] always with all prayer and supplication in the Spirit, being
watchful to this end with all perseverance and supplication for all the
saints—and for me, that utterance may be given to me, that I may open
my mouth boldly to make known the mystery of the Gospel."

The bride of Christ has no restrictions regarding those to whom she evangelizes. She disregards race, color, or creed in her desire to bring glory to God: "therefore those who were scattered went everywhere preaching the word" (Acts 8:4).

The elders who are appointed by God to lead the Church must oversee the preaching, administration of the sacraments, evangelism, discipline, and worship. To place these activities under others is to give up their responsibilities.

The Healthy Church

The Church of Jesus is well-organized at the direction of her Lord so she can fulfill her function of taking the Gospel to the world, producing more offspring. The Reformed understanding, which is solidly biblical, avoids the pitfalls of the hierarchical and the Congregationalist positions.

We must give careful consideration to what we are doing, individually and collectively, within the Church. If the Lord has given us particular gifts, we must use them willingly. If there are some things that we must not do, like appointing a woman as an elder, we must submit to the Word. If we need training for a particular service, we must not delay getting that training, even if it takes a long time.

Surely the Lord's blessings will come on the churches that honor him.

Chapter 7

The Bible

Earlier we mentioned *Sola Scriptura*. This means "the Scriptures alone," or "the Scriptures solely" teach us how to be saved and how to be sanctified. It was one of the most important doctrines associated with the Reformation.

Teaching the doctrines of the Bible caused a great battle for the Reformers in the sixteenth century, because **Roman Catholics believed and taught that the Church's authority was equal to the Scriptures'** authority. **The Roman Catholics also treated traditions as being equal to, or in some cases, greater than the written Word of God.**

Today, some Charismatics follow in the footsteps of Rome insisting that God gives new and direct revelation apart from the Bible. They think that the Bible is not the only authoritative word for what we believe and do. The trouble for the true bride of Christ is that some Christian leaders have been reluctant to challenge this assertion. Christian leaders have been reluctant to do this because they think they might look unspiritual if they questioned some of these "truths" held in high esteem.

In this chapter we will see how we got the Bible, and how the Bible alone teaches what we need for our salvation and service.

General Revelation

General revelation, sometimes called "natural revelation," is what we know from what we observe. We can look at the sky, the human body, and things around us to learn some things about God. The Psalmists spoke of general revelation: "the heavens declare the glory of God; and the firmament shows His handiwork" (Psa 19:1); and Psalm 97:6, "the heavens declare His righteousness, and all the peoples see His glory."

God speaks to all mankind through general revelation. There is no one who can honestly look at the world and truly say that there is no God. Men may deny that there is a Creator, but they know in their hearts they are lying. When we look at something that was made, a table or chair for instance, we know that there was a maker, and so it is with the world. We know that the world was made. More than that, we can know some things about the power and skill of the maker. Paul taught, "since the creation of the world His invisible attributes are clearly seen, being understood by the things that are made, even His eternal power and Godhead, so that they are without excuse" (Rom 1:20).

This knowledge of the existence of God leaves us without excuse if we don't worship God. God would say to the one who refused to serve him: "You have seen my world and know I exist, but you refused to worship me. You have seen how I kept the world from flying off into deep space, you have seen how I controlled the tides and the birds, and you have seen the remarkable predictable workings of science but you refused to worship me." Psalm 19 says that even the deafest person in the world can hear God's voice in his creation. We hear God's words in creation but we shut our ears and hearts to them.

The limitation of natural revelation is that we don't hear of Christ's work as our substitute on the cross for our sins. So how do we know about Christ's redemptive work?

Special Revelation

We learn of Christ's redemptive work through "special revelation." Special revelation is revelation that comes directly from God. Special revelation completes what natural revelation could not. Without special revelation we would never have been able to see how sinful we are. We would never have known how much we needed a Savior. We would never have met the Savior. We would never have known how we are to live as a Christian to please God. We would not know how to worship God. Special revelation is a letter of love from our heavenly Father. Jesus said "the Spirit . . . gives life; the flesh profits nothing. The words that I speak to you are spirit, and they are life" (John 6:63). The ultimate source of special revelation is Jesus Christ. The author of Hebrews told us this: "God, who at various times and in various ways spoke in time past to the fathers by the prophets, has in these last days spoken to us by His Son" (1:1-2a).

In fact, everything in the Bible can trace its ultimate source to Jesus. (By the way, this is why it is unwise to think that "red-lettered" Bibles are better, as if those words have more value than the black-lettered words. All Scriptures come from the Son of God.) Later, the Apostle John confirmed that Jesus is the personification of the Word of God by calling him "the Word of God" in John 1 and Revelation 19.

Without the knowledge of who God is from his Word, we will live horrible lives of sinfulness, groping in darkness. This was how Paul described the Gentiles: "although they knew God, they did not glorify Him as God, nor were thankful, but became futile in their thoughts, and their foolish hearts were darkened. Professing to be wise, they became fools, and changed the glory of the incorruptible God into an image made like corruptible man—and birds and four-footed animals and creeping things" (Rom 1:21-23).

This special revelation that we call the Word of God is unchangeable. We may disagree with it, but it never changes. Not even great assemblies of men have the authority to change, add to, or subtract from the Word of God. Neither are their pronouncements of equal value to God's holy Word. The reason we do not trust their words as being equal to the Bible is that, even though they may have the best of intentions, men are liars and often seek to promote their own self-interests.

Sufficiency of Special Revelation

Paul made it clear in Romans 1 that general revelation is sufficient to leave us without an excuse before God. When we look at the world we know there is a God, and we know we should worship him. But we don't find him or worship him because we are spiritually blinded by our own wickedness. (The fact that we don't and can't look for God is not God's fault but our fault and our ancestors' fault). God is not at fault for us remaining under the condemnation of sin. Now let us focus on the sufficiency of special revelation.

God's Word, his special revelation, sufficiently shows us how to be saved. We learn how wicked we are, and we learn how good God is to choose us and redeem us in Jesus. We learn how God gives us faith, and we learn how to use that faith to receive what Christ offers us - his life and death. In short, we learn how we can receive God's salvation. John was very clear about the purpose of his writing: "these are written that you may believe that Jesus is the Christ, the Son of God, and that believing you may have life in His name" (John 20:31). Paul echoed John: "For I am not ashamed of the Gospel of Christ, for it is the power of God to salvation for everyone who believes, for the Jew first and also for the Greek" (Rom 1:16), also saying "from childhood you have known the Holy Scriptures, which are able to make you wise for salvation through faith which is in Christ Jesus" (2 Tim 3:15).

God's special revelation is sufficient to instruct us how we are sanctified and secured till we go to heaven. We learn how God cleans us up now and gives us directions about how to live and please him. **Without special revelation we would be lost in darkness**. But the light of Jesus gives us direction. Peter exhorts us to "therefore . . . as newborn babes, desire the pure milk of the word, that you may grow thereby" (1 Pet 2:1), and Jesus prayed "sanctify them by Your truth. Your word is truth" (John 17:17). These truths are not confined to the New Testament—"Your word is a lamp to my feet And a light to my path" (Psa 119:105).

God's special revelation is especially necessary at a time of changing values, in this relativistic society. God's Word gives light in dark times. We remember what happened during the time of the Judges: Everyone did what was right in his own eyes. Homosexuality, rape, corruption, injustice, idol worship, adultery, and bloodshed were the order of the day. Without God's Word at the center of their lives, the foundation of Christianity disappeared. In contrast to what is "right in man's eyes," is what is "right in God's eyes." We only see what is "right in God's eyes" when we look at God's Word. Consider two more passages on the blessings of special revelation:

- 2 Timothy 3:16-17 "**All Scripture is given by inspiration of God**, and is profitable for doctrine, for reproof, for correction, for instruction in righteousness, **that the man of God may be complete**, thoroughly equipped for every good work."
- 1 Corinthians 10:11, "Now all these things happened to them as examples, and **they were written for our admonition,** upon whom the ends of the ages have come."

In 1 Corinthians 10, the Apostle Paul not only reminded us how vital all of Scripture is, but he also pointed out that those who looked elsewhere for instruction would run into difficulty. Wouldn't the world be much better if men knew, believed, and obeyed the Word of God? We might be a Prime Minister, president, judge, businessman, diplomat, teacher, or pastor, but only God's Word must guide what we must believe and how we must live. We are not free to ignore God's Word.

We must therefore guard against churches that emphasize singing or entertainment at the expense of the preaching of the Word, and **we must guard against churches that promote the use of the Bible as a list of morals to follow, rather than emphasizing the life and sacrifice of the Lord Jesus Christ**.

Because we have the sufficient and completed Word of God today we should not expect, nor do we need dreams, or any other kind of revelation. And we don't have to worry if we have a dream, wondering if were from God, from the devil, or from bad food we had the night before. Whatever God wanted preserved, it was written down and preserved in the 66 books of the Bible, a book that is now complete.

Roman Catholics have a different view of the Bible. They believe that the Bible needs the Church to give it authority. This is one of the reasons Roman Catholics did not allow their members to have the Bible in their own language. On the contrary, the Reformers required that the Bible be available in the common language for the ordinary man to be able to read. The church needs the Bible. The Bible does not need the Church to become God's authoritative Word. The Word of God gets its authority from God, not from the Church.

How Can We Know That the Bible is True?

First of all, we can know that the Bible is true when we read it. **A sure cure for doubting the Scriptures is to open them and see for ourselves if they were not true.**

We also must ask God for his Holy Spirit to help us to understand and believe the truth in the Bible. When we sincerely ask, God's Holy Spirit will help us. Without him we cannot receive the things which are in God's Word—"But the natural man does not receive the things of the Spirit of God, for they are foolishness to him; nor can he know them, because they are spiritually discerned" (1 Cor 2:14).

The Bible proves that it is true by its dignity and authority. Another word for this is the "self-authentication" of Scripture—the *"autopistia."* We see dignity and authority by the accurateness of the Bible and the excellence of the Bible. The Apostle Paul confirmed that the Bible was not just a general book, but one through which men find hope. Speaking of the Old Testament, he said "whatever things were written before were written for our learning, that we through the patience and comfort of the Scriptures might have hope" (Rom 15:4).

Furthermore, no prophecy of the Bible has ever failed to come true. Consider how the Bible predicted the falls of Egypt, Assyria,

Babylon, Medo-Persia, Greece, and Rome before they happened. And many of those prophecies were made when those nations were not even considered nations, and when they were hardly threats to anyone. Details written about the Greek Empire in particular, given years before Greece was ever a recognized world force, were remarkably accurate. Consider another example of the accuracy of the Bible—the remarkable details of prophecies concerning Christ's parents, life, death, resurrection, ascension, friends, betrayer, etc. It is unimaginable that those prophecies could have referred to anyone else but Jesus.

There is an important application that we must not miss here. When we see the confirmations of past truths and of God's power to fulfill what he promised, it is easier to trust God when he speaks of future things. For example, knowing God's truthfulness, won't we confidently expect and wait for Christ's return to take his saints to be with him at the end of the world?

The Source of Revelation

God spoke in many ways to give special revelation.

- **Theophanies were Christ's appearances in the Old Testament to people like Abraham, Jacob, Samson's parents, and Gideon.**

We see the Lord appearing in Genesis 32:28-30, speaking to Jacob:

He said, 'Your name shall no longer be called Jacob, but Israel; for you have struggled with God and with men, and have prevailed.' Then Jacob asked, saying, 'Tell me Your name, I pray.' And He said, 'Why is it that you ask about My name?' And He blessed him there. And Jacob called the name of the place Peniel: 'For I have seen God face to face, and my life is preserved.'

Another example is in Judges 6:22-24—"Now Gideon perceived that He was the Angel of the LORD. So Gideon said, 'Alas, O Lord GOD! For I have seen the Angel of the LORD face to face.' Then the LORD said to him, 'Peace be with you; do not fear, you shall not die.' So Gideon built an altar there to the LORD, and called it The-LORD-Is-Peace. To this day it is still in Ophrah of the Abiezrites."

- **Prophecies.** God caused people to say certain things that he wanted man to hear.

Men spoke, but the words were the words of God. Hebrews 1:1-2b captures the idea: "God, who at various times and in various ways spoke in time past to the fathers by the prophets, has in these last days spoken to us by His Son." As God spoke to his prophets through these various means, he moved godly men to write them down, like Peter said, "prophecy never came by the will of man, but holy men of God spoke as they were moved by the Holy Spirit" (2 Pet 1:21).

God's Word was so powerful that it moved men to write even when they were reluctant. Jeremiah, for instance, wanted to stop speaking the Words (prophecies) of God because men tried to kill him for it. His feeling was so strong that he wished he were not born. But he could not stop speaking God's truth. He cried,

> O LORD, You induced me, and I was persuaded; You are stronger than I, and have prevailed. I am in derision daily; everyone mocks me. For when I spoke, I cried out; I shouted, 'Violence and plunder!' Because the word of the LORD was made to me a reproach and a derision daily. Then I said, 'I will not make mention of Him, nor speak anymore in His name.' But His word was in my heart like a burning fire shut up in my bones; I was weary of holding it back, and I could not (Jer 20:7-9).

Amos said a similar thing. He knew that when God spoke he had had to speak: "surely the Lord GOD does nothing, unless He reveals His secret to His servants the prophets. A lion has roared! Who will not fear? The Lord GOD has spoken! Who can but prophesy?" (Amos 3:7-8).

- **Dreams were night visions that had to be interpreted**.

For example, God appeared to Jacob as he ran away from Esau and gave him revelation by a dream—"Then he dreamed, and behold, a ladder was set up on the earth, and its top reached to heaven; and there the angels of God were ascending and descending on it. And behold, the LORD stood above it and said: 'I am the LORD God of Abraham your father and the

God of Isaac; the land on which you lie I will give to you and your descendants'" (Gen 28:12-13).

As one more example, Daniel said he wrote down what God showed him in his dreams: "In the first year of Belshazzar king of Babylon, Daniel had a dream and visions of his head while on his bed. Then he wrote down the dream, telling the main facts" (Dan 7:1).

- **Visions were direct revelations of the mind**. They did not need to be interpreted.

For instance, in Genesis 15:1, Abram had a vision—"After these things the word of the LORD came to Abram in a vision, saying, 'Do not be afraid, Abram. I am your shield, your exceedingly great reward.'"

- **Angels brought messages from God to his people.**

We see them in many cases especially in the Old Testament, and we see them again when Jesus was announced to Mary, Joseph, and the shepherds of Bethlehem.

- **Jesus himself**. Jesus spoke in person in the New Testament; John 1:1-2 and Hebrews 1:1-2 point to the authoritative revelations of Jesus.

- **Jesus's Apostles or their close associates wrote Scriptures**. The Apostle Peter confirmed that the Apostle Paul wrote Scripture when he said
  Consider that the longsuffering of our Lord is salvation—as also our beloved brother Paul, according to the wisdom given to him, has written to you, as also in all his epistles, speaking in them of these things, in which are some things hard to understand, which untaught and unstable people twist to their own destruction, **as they do also <u>the rest</u> of the Scriptures** (2 Peter 3:15-16).

Everything God wanted us to have from past special revelation (Old Testament), he has preserved and passed down. They were then joined to special revelation from Jesus and his Apostles, or their close associates. All these writings together are the Bible, the completed canon, the Word of God. Because God's Word was completed, it is sufficient to teach us everything we need to know (2 Tim 3:15-17).

This whole process of God giving his Word to us through men is called "inspiration." Inspiration means "God-breathed." The words of the Bible were breathed out by God. But how did God move men to write? God used writers with their own particular talents, struggles, feeling, and circumstances to write down his words. This is why we see some personality characteristics and some details of places and times recorded in the Bible. For example, Luke was a doctor and showed his medical training in his writing. He often gave details of medical conditions. Peter reflects his simple fisherman nature by writing with a simpler style. Amos, the shepherd and farmer, talked of figs and animals.

Why did God want man to write down his Word? Why not simply memorize what God wanted man to know? God caused men to write down what he taught them because it was more durable and reliable. We know what happens when twenty people have to pass on a story in sequence. It changes dramatically. God wanted to preserve his Word.

Which Books Are to Be in the Bible?

When we speak of the canon of Scripture, we mean the books which are included in the Bible. It is important to know which books are in the canon, as the Bible is our only guide for what we believe and how we live. If we don't know which books are in the canon we can be deceived by false books which will rob us of the true knowledge of God. Then we wouldn't be able to properly know how to serve him.

First, **Jesus confirmed that the thirty-nine books of the Old Testament were part of the canon**. Jesus and his Apostles often quoted from the Old Testament as Scriptures. How do we see Jesus's confirmation? In Luke 11:51 Jesus says "from the blood of Abel to the blood of Zechariah who perished between the altar and the temple. Yes, I say to you, it shall be required of this generation." You see, Abel was mentioned in the first book of the Bible, in Genesis 4. Zechariah was mentioned in the last written book of the Old Testament, in 2 Chronicles

24:20-24. The Old Testament books in Hebrew were put in a different order from ours. 2 Chronicles was the last book of the Old Testament in the Hebrew original. It was an attempt to have the books in chronological order. **More specifically, Jesus confirmed the established books of the Old Testament by their categories**. There were three categories: the law, which consisted of the first five books of the Old Testament, the Psalms, which included all of the poetic books, and the prophets, which included all the rest.

He claimed that all three categories of the Old Testament were written about him, saying, "These are the words which I spoke to you while I was still with you, that all things must be fulfilled which were written in the Law of Moses and the Prophets and the Psalms concerning Me." (Luke 24:44-45).

The Apostle Paul appealed to the Old Testament, confirming that they were part of the Scriptures, teaching "whatever things were written before were written for our learning, that we, through the patience and comfort of the Scriptures, might have hope" (Rom 15:4).

We can read about Malachi, Isaiah, Joel, Hosea, Zechariah, and many others in the New Testament where they were confirmed as parts of the Bible. What about the New Testament? How can we know which books are legitimately in it? First, we can look at God's Word to help confirm which books ought and ought not to be in the canon of the New Testament. For example, in Apostle Paul's letter to the Colossians he authoritatively required that that letter be read to the neighboring churches and vice versa. (Col 4:16). As an Apostle, he had the authority to write God's Word as he was moved by the Holy Spirit.

Second, the **Apostle Peter confirmed that Paul's writings were part of the canon,** as we saw above. He called Paul's writings "Scriptures," equating them with the Old Testament (2 Pet 3:15-17).

Third, and ultimately, **it was up to God to determine which books were to be included in the canon**. Man did not decide on it. For instance, the Apostle Paul wrote at least sixteen books, but only thirteen were preserved by God. The Church simply received what God preserved. In AD 397 the Church officially recognized the 66 books of

the Bible. They used the following standards to determine which books
were parts of the Bible.

a. That the book was preserved by God.

**b. That the book was written by an Apostle or his close
associate.**

c. That the book was already widely used in the churches.

The Church recognized the 66 books of the Bible: 39 in the Old
Testament, and 27 in the New Testament. Some sects have rejected this
and added books that they decided should be in the Canon.

Errors Refuted: The Bible

There are many errors concerning the doctrine of the Scriptures.
This is not surprising as the doctrine of Scriptures is one of the most
attacked doctrines of the modern era.

- Error: The Bible is not sufficient; we need more revelation.

First, the Bible directly claims to be sufficient, where Paul writes
"all Scripture is given by inspiration of God, and is profitable for
doctrine, for reproof, for correction, for instruction in righteousness,
<u>that</u> the man of God **may be complete, thoroughly equipped for
every good work**" (2 Tim 3:16-17).

Second, it is illogical to want to have more revelation if we
already have the completed Word of God. Earlier in history, before the
Bible was completed, God spoke through dreams, visions, angels,
prophets, and providential circumstances, but now he speaks through his
Word. The primitive ways of speaking in the past passed away when the
written Word of God was completed. Remember again what is said in
Hebrews 1:1-2: "God, who at various times and in various ways spoke in
time past to the fathers by the prophets, has in these last days spoken to
us by His Son, whom He has appointed heir of all things, through whom
also He made the worlds." The earlier ways of communicating to man
were like dim lights. When the brighter light came, the dimmer ones
became unnecessary. Paul alludes to this in 1 Corinthians 13:9-10, "for

we know in part and we prophesy in part. But when that which is perfect has come, then that which is in part will be done away."

Those dimmer lights were sufficient for their times, but now we have the whole, written Word of God. No one can add to that which is completed. Who can add more water to a cup that is full? Is it possible to add a fifth door to a 4-door car? If someone wants to argue that we need more revelation from God, then he needs to ask himself: How can I add to that which is complete? Further, in 2 Timothy 3:17, the Apostle Paul does not say that the man of God may be **partly equipped** for every good work by the Word of God; Paul said that the man of God is **thoroughly equipped** for every good work by the Word of God.

I believe it was theologian John Owen summarized the sufficiency of Scripture and the subsequent elimination of the need to have new revelation in this way: "If private revelations agree with the Scriptures, they are needless; if they disagree, they are false."

Third, when we know that the Scriptures are sufficient, we won't have uncertainty about what we should do—everything is there in the Word of God. A man said to me once: "I want to do for God what my gut tells me." But God does not want us to go on our "gut feeling," because feelings have been corrupted by sin. Another preacher said: "I will not work under anyone except when the Holy Spirit tells me." By doing this he rejected the Bible as the authoritative Word of God. The Holy Spirit gave us God's Word, and the Word says that elders govern the Church. That preacher should submit to his elders. God wants us to believe and live according to his authoritative Word, which he has given to us. God wants to relieve frustration in his children. What care! What comfort to us!

There is a limit to what God has revealed, however; observe: "the secret things belong to the LORD our God, but those things which are revealed belong to us and to our children forever, that we may do all the words of this law" (Deut 29:29). This is important because sometimes, especially in the modern Charismatic movement, there are some who want to know more, or they want to know things ahead of time. They ignore the fact that prophecies and the like were given because God's Word wasn't completed yet. Some may think that prophecies were given as a form of Christian astrology, predicting their future, but we must remember that prophecies were simply the revealed mind of God. They were not necessarily predictive of the future—prophecy's first goal was to be instructive of God's will.

- Error: There are more than 66 books in my Bible.

Roman Catholics added some books, called the Apocrypha, to the canon. Apocrypha means "of unknown origin" or "hidden." The Christian Church has never received these books as part of the God-inspired Bible. What makes the Roman Catholic error worse is that while they add the Apocryphal books to the Bible, they reject other parts of the present Bible. Let me give you an example. Roman Catholics teach that Mary was perfect, born sinless, and they call her the "Queen of Heaven." Yet the Bible says that all men (and women) were born in sin. **Even Mary pointed out her own sin by showing her need for salvation: "my spirit has rejoiced in God my Savior**. For He has regarded the lowly state of His maidservant; for behold, henceforth all generations will call me blessed" (Luke 1:47-48).

Muslims believe that in addition to the Old and New Testaments, God gave them a new revelation. They argue that the Word of God became corrupt, and God had to send the Koran, which Allah managed to keep pure. (They think God failed to keep the Bible pure.) Yet, a good student of the Word of God will find remarkable preservation of the purity and inerrancy of the Word of God, which have further been confirmed by the Dead Sea Scrolls.

Mormons, Jehovah's Witnesses, Seventh Day Adventists and other cults also have a problem with the sufficiency of the Bible. They place other books alongside the Bible, even when they contain statements that contradict the Bible.

Charismatics probably make the strongest attacks against the sufficiency of the Bible. They believe that God's Holy Spirit speaks today through speaking in tongues (though they usually don't offer any translations, as the Scriptures require in 1 Corinthians 14), prophecies, and words of wisdom and words of knowledge. For many, "speaking in tongues" is more of a status symbol than anything of value to the churches, but when Charismatics rely on supposed revelations like prophecies from the Holy Spirit, what they think the Holy Spirit is telling them then goes beyond the Word of God. Their understanding becomes the final authority. On the other hand, **if their supposed revelations are consistent with the Bible, then why would they need those "new revelations" in the first place**? Why won't they simply study the Bible? I refer you back to John Owen's quote above.

The warnings from God in Revelation, Deuteronomy, and Galatians are most appropriate at this point. God does not look kindly on anyone who tries to add to his Word.

- Revelation 22:18-19, "I testify to everyone who hears the words of the prophecy of this book: **If anyone adds to these things, God will add to him the plagues that are written in this book**; and if anyone takes away from the words of the book of this prophecy, God shall take away his part from the Book of Life, from the holy city, and from the things which are written in this book."

- Deuteronomy 4:2, "**You shall not add to the word which I command you**, nor take from it, that you may keep the commandments of the LORD your God which I command you."

The Apostle Paul strictly warned the churches to reject anyone who brought any other Gospel than that which they heard. In fact, he condemned to hell those who would do that: "**But even if we, or an angel from heaven, preach any other Gospel to you than what we have preached to you, let him be accursed**" (Gal 1:8).

- Error: There are 66 books in the Bible but some are not very useful.

Anabaptists, people who are somewhat related to modern Baptists, believed that the Old Testament books were more or less useless because the God of the Old Testament was an angry God who always brought judgment on people. They believed that the New Testament books were valid because they spoke of grace. They were wrong on both points. The Old Testament is full of grace and prefigured the completion of that grace in Christ's sacrifice on the cross. Abraham was saved by grace through faith in Jesus Christ, as were all the saints in the Old and New Testament periods. **All Old Testament saints heard and believed the same Gospel**.

Look at one example of the Gospel of Jesus Christ in Isaiah. Philip the deacon preached Christ to the Ethiopian eunuch before the New Testament was written, in Acts 8:34-35: "So the eunuch answered Philip and said, 'I ask you, of whom does the prophet say this, of himself or of some other man?' Then Philip opened his mouth, and beginning at this Scripture, preached Jesus to him." Also, in **Hebrews 11, which is called the "faith chapter" of the Bible, the author confirms that Old Testament believers, just as New Testament believers, had faith in Jesus Christ**. Look at one example: "By faith Moses, when he became of age, refused to be called the son of Pharaoh's daughter, choosing rather to suffer affliction with the people of God than to enjoy the passing pleasures of sin, esteeming the reproach of Christ greater riches than the treasures in Egypt; for he looked to the reward" (Hebrews 11:24-26). **Hebrews 12:1-2 also confirms that the Old Testament saints' faith was in Jesus**. The Apostle Paul taught in Ephesians 2 that Jews and Gentiles were members of the same Church. We can confidently say that for both Old and New Testaments, the glory of God and the salvation of man were the focus.

When someone says that the Old Testament books lack grace, this is man's misunderstanding of them. Remember Jesus's words from Luke 24—the law, the prophets, and the Psalms spoke of him. He exemplified and brought grace.

The Old Testament books are full of God's grace and truth. Christ's life and work are taught and pictured everywhere in them. Solomon spoke of the futility of life apart from Jesus Christ in Ecclesiastes. He spoke of God's love for his Bride and those who would join his Bride in Song of Solomon. David spoke of the expansion of Christ's kingdom and his triumph over his enemies. Isaac was promised grace through his Seed (Galatians 3:16), and the Apostle Paul made clear the Seed was Jesus Christ. Isaac was assured that all nations of the earth would be blessed through his Seed.

Love the Bible!

God's Word teaches you everything you need to know about yourself, about God, about your salvation, and about how you should live now.

You must constantly take time to refresh your knowledge of God. Other books might help, but you have to guard against many writers who pretend to speak for God, who use the Bible as a means of making money, or who are deceived themselves. If you take time to study the Bible you will be like the ant who saves up food for winter in summer. Of course, you must always ask God for his Holy Spirit to help you clearly understand the Word of God. When you study the Word of God you show how much you love God and your neighbor.

These words from Psalm 19 should reflect your own desire for the Word of God: "The judgments of the LORD are true and righteous altogether. More to be desired are they than gold, yea, than much fine gold; sweeter also than honey and the honeycomb. Moreover by them Your servant is warned, and in keeping them there is great reward" (Psa 19:9b-11). Of note in this passage is that the judgments of God refer to the first 5 books of the Bible.

Be sure to imitate the Psalmist in meditating on God's Word: "Oh, how I love Your law! It is my meditation all the day" (Psa 119:97).

Listen carefully to preaching. Take notes if that helps. Discuss the sermon the Pastor preaches with your wife and children. Obey God's Word and grow in grace. Tell it to others. Give it to others. Worship the God who gave you his Word.

What sadness if someone refuses to open God's love letter and never learns of salvation and sanctification in Christ Jesus!

Chapter 8

Covenant and Baptism

Most of us accept that those who profess faith in Jesus Christ need to join the church, and in order to join the church, they need to be baptized. Jesus explicitly commanded this.

Matthew 28:19 - Go therefore and make disciples of all the nations, baptizing them in the name of the Father and of the Son and of the Holy Spirit...

But while we generally agree on the need for baptism, there are notable differences between the Reformed position and what many churches hold today. So we will examine these differences in this chapter.

Believers and Their Children Were Part of the Old Covenant

Believers and their children were part of the covenant community (the Church) in the Old Testament. This is beyond doubt. Yes, children surely could not express their faith or even understand faith, but they were part of the covenant community. The parents showed that their children were part of the community by the covenant sign of circumcision, being put on their male children. Parents put this mark on covenant children at the direction of God in Genesis

17:7, "I will establish My covenant between Me and you and your descendants after you in their generations, for an everlasting covenant, to be God to you and your descendants after you," where he went on to command "every male child among you shall be circumcised; and you shall be circumcised in the flesh of your foreskins, and it shall be a sign of the covenant between Me and you" (Gen 17:11). Furthermore, those who refused the sign of the covenant were marked for death: "he who is born in your house and he who is bought with your money must be circumcised, and My covenant shall be in your flesh for an everlasting covenant. And the uncircumcised male child, who is not circumcised in the flesh of his foreskin, that person shall be cut off from his people; he has broken My covenant" (Gen 17:13-14).

God showed his covenant blessings on his covenant children when they were saved by their fathers, who painted the blood of the Passover lamb on their doorposts before they left Egypt. Those children might have been infants without faith, but they were saved by their parents' faith that the parents expressed publicly with the blood on their doorposts. The Angel of Death passed over them and did no harm to the covenant children, but the Egyptians families lost their firstborn sons (Ex 12:26-27). God did not let his covenant children die in Pharaoh's Egypt.

God directly addressed children as members of the covenant, showing they are distinct from non-covenant children— "Honor your father and your mother, that your days may be long upon the land which the LORD your God is giving you" (Ex 20:12). This command was covenant law.

God addresses covenant children as his; he does not cast pearls to swine. Covenant children were dear to his heart. Consider Isaiah's words: "All your children shall be taught by the LORD, And great shall be the peace of your children" (Isa 54:13).

In Zechariah 10, we see little children living in the church with the elderly:

> those of Ephraim shall be like a mighty man, and their
> heart shall rejoice as if with wine. Yes, their children shall
> see it and be glad; their heart shall rejoice in the LORD. I

will whistle for them and gather them, for I will redeem them; and they shall increase as they once increased. I will sow them among the peoples, and they shall remember Me in far countries; they shall live, together with their children, and they shall return (Zech 10:7-9).

Parents in the Old Testament showed that their children were part of the community by fulfilling their God-given obligations to them. They taught their children the same Gospel, prayed for them, disciplined them, and made sacrifices for them. They did not allow them to intermarry with pagans. If the children of the Israelites were pagans, God would not have cared if they intermarried with pagans. **But believers in the Old Testament did not treat their children as pagans.**

The condition for inclusion in the covenant was clear: **all the Israelites and foreigners who wanted to join God's people had to put their faith in the coming Savior**. This is the same faith as we have today. You see proof of this in Hebrews 11, which gives a list of believers in the Old Testament who had faith in the Lord Jesus, the same Lord Jesus in whom we put our faith. But to put their faith in Jesus, they had to hear the same Isaiah 53 Gospel that the Ethiopian eunuch heard from Philip—indeed the same message we hear today. This incorporated those who believed into the true Israel—the Church, the same Church as we are in today. To show that they were incorporated into the same true covenant community, they had to show they were committed to covenant keeping. **One of those ways they showed they were committed to the covenant was to allow God to mark their children with the covenant sign, which incorporated those children into the covenant community.** So, we notice that the covenant sign had to do with more than the Jewish boys; it had to do with the parents as well.

When the Jewish boys were circumcised, they were raised by their parents with an awareness of their sins, and taught by their parents to look for and receive their forgiveness through their Covenant Keeper, through faith, in the Lord Jesus Christ. They were also trained to worship God. The children may not have had faith in Jesus Christ, but their parents had faith, and by virtue of the parent's faith, children were incorporated into the covenant community and promised salvation. As those children matured, God required that they claim what they were promised.

To summarize, the Old Testament believers and their children heard the same Gospel, had the same faith, were saved by the same Savior, and were members of the same Church community.

With all these things being the same in the Old and New Testaments, it is logical to expect a covenantal sign to continue for believers and their children. **It would be a most remarkable thing, if, while all conditions remained the same between the Old and New Testaments, the sign would simply be taken away and no mention made of it.**

Believers and Their Children Are Part of the New Covenant

Is there evidence that children in the New Testament are part of the covenant? Yes, there is much evidence to support this.

We see that all believers and their children are part of the covenant in the New Testament when the Covenant Keeper **Jesus treated covenant children as holy**, and put his hands on them to bless them. God does not bless the wicked with spiritual blessings. In fact, he even rebuked those who were trying to chase the children away.[1] Jesus did not tolerate ill-treatment of his covenant children, and he especially did not tolerate ill-treatment of his covenant children from his own disciples. He told his disciples to let his children stay with him and not to send them away. He said, "'let the little children come to Me, and do not forbid them; for of such is the kingdom of heaven.' And He laid His hands on them and departed from there" (Matt 19:14-15).

This is why Reformed churches include children in worship services, and we encourage parents to teach their children at home. This is why we teach our children to pray. I heard a minister once say,

---

1. Mark 10:14 and Luke 18:16.

"Covenant children are not 'vipers in diapers'." We must treat them as covenant children of God. We believe that the sacrifice of Jesus and the faith of our parents in him allow our children to approach the throne of heaven without fear. There is no prayer without the proper sacrifice.

We see that all believers and their children are part of the covenant in the New Testament when the Apostle Peter quoted from the Old Testament to make the same point: children are in the covenant, and have their sins forgiven. He preached "repent, and let every one of you be baptized in the name of Jesus Christ for the remission of sins; and you shall receive the gift of the Holy Spirit. For the promise is to you and to your children, and to all who are afar off, as many as the Lord our God will call" (Acts 2:38-39). Peter does not say the promise is for adults only, or only for those who are old enough to speak for themselves.

We see that all believers and their children are part of the covenant in the New Testament when Gentiles and their families received the promise of salvation and were incorporated into the covenant community. This was what the Apostle Paul said to the Philippian jailer. The jailer's whole family was baptized that night when he believed: "believe on the Lord Jesus Christ, and you will be saved, you and your household" (Acts 16:31). The passage goes on to show "he and all his family were baptized" (Acts 16:33).

We often miss the phrase "and your household" when we read Acts 16:31. Notice how the Apostle Paul did not say that the members of the Philippian jailer's household would be saved when they were old enough to believe for themselves.

We see that all believers and their children are part of the covenant in the New Testament when Jesus declared that Zacchaeus' household received salvation when he believed: "and Jesus said to him, 'Today salvation has come to this house, because he also is a son of Abraham; for the Son of Man has come to seek and to save that which was lost'" (Luke 19:9-10). "House" was referring to the people in the house, not the building.

To be clear, the Bible does not teach that every single person becomes a Christian where a parent becomes a Christian. This was a promise in general. Remember how God says that if children honor their parents they would dwell long in Canaan? That was a covenantal promise. Surely not all the Israelite children honored their parents during the time that Israel occupied Canaan. Zacchaeus and others received the covenant promise, and they had to train their children to claim it. When their children claimed it, they were saved.

We see that all believers and their children are part of the covenant in the New Testament when Luke reiterated that Lydia's whole family was incorporated into the Church. The sign of the covenant was applied to all of them. This was proof of their incorporation into the covenant community. Luke reports

> A certain woman named Lydia heard us. She was a seller of purple from the city of Thyatira, who worshiped God. The Lord opened her heart to heed the things spoken by Paul. And when she and her household were baptized, she begged us, saying, 'If you have judged me to be faithful to the Lord, come to my house and stay' (Acts 16:14-15).

We see that all believers and their children are part of the covenant in the New Testament when Stephanas' whole family was baptized and brought into the covenant community. The Apostle Paul confirmed that he baptized them, saying "Yes, I also baptized the household of Stephanas. Besides, I do not know whether I baptized any other" (1 Cor 1:16).

Never was it recorded that a child of believing parents was baptized when he "came of age." Yes, we must be careful when we argue from silence, but it is reasonable to conclude this when we consider that whole households were baptized. It would have been most remarkable as well that none of these families who were baptized had any young children, particularly considering that some had to be younger parents by virtue of their work.

We see that all believers and their children are part of the covenant community in the New Testament when God specifically declared that children of believers were holy. Since God made the family the center of the covenant, and since children are in the family, they are included in the covenant and are distinguished from the world.

Surely there is a qualitative difference between children of believers and non-believers, and so they ought to be baptized. Covenant blessings in the family unquestionably flow to the other members. "For the unbelieving husband is sanctified by the wife, and the unbelieving wife is sanctified by the husband; otherwise your children would be unclean, but now they are holy" (1 Cor 7:14).

Even spouses of believers (not children only) were considered holy. On the other hand, Baptists view children as pagans who are in danger of hell fire. But as you see, the Apostle Paul did not see it that way, and rejected that notion under the inspiration of the Holy Spirit. He taught that the covenant signs declared children of believers to be holy and filled with the promises of God. He taught this based on the fact that those who were not given the mark were excluded from the Old Testament assembly and even killed. This is illustrated for us in in Leviticus 14, where the leper, because of his uncleanness, was excluded (literally, cut off) from the assembly of God's people so that the people would be clean. In short, Baptists view children as wicked, and so they exclude children from the covenant. They view their children as being in a worse place under the "new" covenant than under the "old" covenant. Reformed believers view their children as holy and include them in the covenant.

We view our children as in the same privileged position as in the Old Testament, not in a worse position.

Now while we may not presume that all our children will be saved simply because they are part of the covenant, (for the covenant doesn't save) neither must we presume as our Baptist brothers do that our children are under condemnation. **Instead, based on God's command and promises, we baptize our children, we treat our children as holy, and we fulfill our responsibilities to them**.

There are some who reject God's covenant sign for children out of ignorance. They argue like this: "God called the covenant with Abraham 'a covenant of circumcision' but now we have 'a covenant of grace.' This means the old covenant has passed and now we have a new covenant with new rules." The reason they are wrong is this: God only used the phrase "covenant of circumcision" to identify that covenant.

<u>**The requirement of the covenant has always been to have faith in the coming Savior**</u>, as you saw above. (Examples: The SALT treaty has nothing to do with salt or the Kyoto Protocol has nothing to do with Kyoto. They were both names only.) We have the same covenant as Abraham. We both believe in Christ's sacrifice for our sins. We have the same faith as him. We are incorporated into the same covenant community as him.

This should leave us beyond doubt that both believers and their children are part of the covenant throughout the history of the Church. This continues today.

Believers and Their Children Must Have a Sign of the Covenant

Based on God's command, all believers and their children must have a covenant sign. Adults are baptized based on their faith, and children are baptized based on the faith of their parents. The baptism of children is like a down payment on their salvation. Children must claim the balance when they are old enough to speak for themselves; of course, if those children died in childhood or in the womb, the Lord is well able to save them based on their parents' faith. After all, if God condemned them because of their parents' sin before they were born, he could save them on account of their parents' faith before they were born or while they are children.

All believers and their children must have a covenant sign because the covenant sign was intended to be an assurance of God's love for believers and their children. In baptism God reminds us (with a perfect sign) and assures us (with a permanent seal) that he has fully paid for all our sins, and that we belong to him 100% forever. Baptism is not a simple ritual that the Lord wants us to go through. It is more than a sign: baptism assures us that our souls were marked "property of Christ."

A man proves he loves his bride by assuring her of his love, by publicly displaying his love and giving his wife a ring. The ring does not make the marriage, but the ring is the regular assurance of his love for his bride! The ring tells the world that the bride's husband loves her. Similarly, in baptism Christ displays the regular assurance of his love for his bride, the Church.

All believers and their children must have a covenant sign because those who refuse to submit themselves or their children to baptism are in open rebellion against the Lord. They show a dismissive attitude to what Christ did on the cross. This was a sin of the prophet Moses, seen in Exodus 4:24-26:

> And it came to pass on the way, at the encampment, that the LORD met him and sought to kill him. Then Zipporah took a sharp stone and cut off the foreskin of her son and cast it at Moses' feet, and said, 'Surely you are a husband of blood to me!' So He let him go. Then she said, 'You are a husband of blood!' — because of the circumcision.

Here God was about to kill Moses, to kill the one who was going to lead God's people to the Promised Land, because he had not applied the covenant sign to his son. **It is a sign of great arrogance to refuse to put the sign of the covenant on a covenant child.** If God includes children into the covenant and puts his covenant sign on them, we must not dare exclude them. To reject the sign of baptism on a child is to rob God of the honor that should come to him. It also robs the child of the precious position and promises God has reserved for him.

All believers and their children must have a covenant sign, because neither Jesus nor his disciples revoked a sign of the covenant on children. In the New Testament we are told not to make sacrifices anymore. We are told that we are no longer restricted in what animals we eat. We are told that temple trips to Jerusalem are no longer necessary. We are told that Christians are not to make sacrifices any longer. But we are never told to stop putting the mark of the covenant on our children. If the disciples wanted to exclude them they would have said so. <u>Those who think that their children have no need of and</u>

ought not to have the sign of the covenant have the burden of
proof. They must prove that God has revoked the sign of the covenant
on children and has put the children out of the covenant, even while so
much else remains the same.

All believers and their children must have a covenant sign
because God requires that we enter into covenant with him by taking the
sign of the covenant on us and our children. God entered into covenant
with us. We did not ask for the covenant, but we are thankful that the
Lord entered into covenant with us. So, it is not up to us to decide
whether or not we should baptize our children.

As you can see, Reformed Christians take a God-ward view of
baptism, while Arminians take a man-ward view of baptism. Arminians
reject infant baptism because they believe that baptism is a sign of human
faith (man-ward). With the Arminian view, little children cannot be
baptized because they have no faith and are not able to make any
commitment to God. But when we have a God-ward view of baptism,
and we see baptism as God's grace towards us in Christ, the spiritual level
of the person being baptized is not the issue. This is also why Reformed
ministers would baptize an older person who might have a diminished
mental capacity or is otherwise handicapped.

But Which Sign Should Believers and Their Children Have Today?

Believers and their children should be baptized with water.
Since the bloody sign of circumcision was no longer appropriate, being
fulfilled in Jesus's death, God changed the sign. God had to change the
sign. The signs that God gave to his covenant children have often been
called "sensible signs." They are called "sensible signs" because there is
clear logic to God's decisions. God never gave random signs. For sure,
God did not change the thing signified by the sign—the removal of our
sins through blood—but he only changed the sign to one that was more
appropriate.

How did Christ fulfill the sign of circumcision? To get the answer we must consider what circumcision was in the first place. Circumcision was the cutting off of the male foreskin that fell to the ground and died. This was accompanied with the shedding of blood. As a result of circumcision, the child was made clean. **This was a picture of Christ Christ's bloody death. His blood would fall to the ground, he would die, and we would become clean**.

Paul makes it abundantly clear that Christ was our circumcision in Colossians 2:11-12 "in Him you were also circumcised with the circumcision made without hands, by putting off the body of the sins of the flesh, by the circumcision of Christ, buried with Him in baptism, in which you also were raised with Him through faith in the working of God, who raised Him from the dead."

So, Christ's bloody death fulfilled what was pictured by circumcision. It no longer made sense to have a bloody covenant sign but that we should have a non-bloody covenant sign. The Lord gave us water baptism as the covenant sign.

How Do We Deal with Baptized Covenant Children?

We must not be presumptive about our children's salvation (as some Reformed people are), acting as if God would save our children simply because they are in the covenant and have been baptized.

We must not be presumptive as the Baptists, treating our children as rebellious pagans who have no hope until they can speak for themselves.

We are called to teach our children about what the Lord Jesus has done for them so they can receive his promises by faith. The baptism of a child is like a check—a promise to pay. Only when you believe a check is good and take it to the bank will you receive the benefits of it. You need to respond to your baptism in faith, and receive the salvation God promised you. This is why Esau, who received the sign of the covenant, went to hell and Jacob went to heaven. **It is the job of the parents to** teach their children the Word of God so that they can be brought to faith in Jesus.

We are called to pray with and for our children. We must also teach our children to pray. It is inconsistent, but welcomed, when a Baptist brother teaches his child to pray. Logically, if a child is unregenerate he has no access to God. (There is no prayer without the sacrifice of Jesus). But the reality is, the brother is right to teach his child to pray.

We are called to discipline our children when they stray from the path of righteousness in order that they might return. If we let our children go the way they want, because of the natural rebellion in their hearts, they will stray.

We are called to worship with our children. Sing with your children: "Jesus loves the little children" and "Jesus loves me this I know." Claim the Lord's promise to you and your household.

Mode of Baptism

Let us touch briefly on the mode (the method) of baptism as there is a fair amount of disagreement on this topic.

There are some who argue that being buried with Christ was a symbol of the mode of baptism. They passionately believe and teach that baptism must only be done by immersion, not by sprinkling or pouring, as the Reformers taught. Paul said, "we were buried with Him through baptism into death, that just as Christ was raised from the dead by the glory of the Father, even so we also should walk in newness of life" (Rom 6:4). It is possible, with this verse existing in isolation, to come to this conclusion that baptism must be by immersion. But we must, now and always, consider the context.

Why is context so important? Consider one example from a parable Jesus spoke about Lazarus and the rich man in Luke 16. From reaching that passage of Scripture, we might think that there are conversations between people in heaven and hell after this world is over. No! That parable was not intending to teach that. Rather, it was intending to teach that people must preach and people must hear and believe the Gospel now.

So, let us look at the whole context of Romans 6:4. Baptism in this context was referring to being "united" or "joined" with Christ. It was not referring to the mode of baptism. Paul was referring to the unity between believers and Christ in his life, death, burial, and resurrection. Look at the fuller context—

> Or do you not know that as many of us as were baptized
> into Christ Jesus were baptized into His death? Therefore
> we were buried with Him through baptism into death,
> that just as Christ was raised from the dead by the glory of
> the Father, even so we also should walk in newness of life.
> For if we have been united together in the likeness of His
> death, certainly we also shall be in the likeness of His
> resurrection, knowing this, that our old man was crucified
> with Him, that the body of sin might be done away with,
> that we should no longer be slaves of sin.

We notice that the Apostle Paul was speaking of the basis on which we receive the benefits of Jesus. We had to be united with him to receive his benefits. We were in him when he died, so we died. We were in him when he was buried, so we were buried. And we were in him when he was resurrected, so we are raised. Further, this section of Romans was dealing with how we are saved. (Romans 1-3 is about how sinful we are; Romans 4-11, how we are saved from our sins; and Romans 12-16, how we serve God after being set free.)

Jesus similarly used the term "baptism" to express unity— but unity in suffering—

> But Jesus said to them, 'You do not know what you ask.
> Are you able to drink the cup that I drink, and be
> baptized with the baptism that I am baptized with?' They
> said to Him, 'We are able.' So Jesus said to them, 'You
> will indeed drink the cup that I drink, and with the
> baptism I am baptized with you will be baptized' (Mark
> 10:38-39).

Jesus was not speaking of the mode of baptism. Jesus wasn't asking his disciples to be baptized. They were already baptized. Jesus was using "baptism" in a figurative way. He was speaking of believers being united with him in his suffering. You can confirm this with the parallel application in Verse 39: "Are you able to drink the cup [of suffering] that I drink…"

On the other hand, if Baptists want to use the argument that because we are buried with Christ we must therefore be immersed, they will have a hard time explaining how we "put on" Christ in baptism: "for as many of you as were baptized into Christ have put on Christ" (Gal 3:27). This sounds like something coming from above. The sounds more like sprinkling or pouring.

Further, our Baptist brothers will have a hard time explaining how the Holy Spirit came on the heads of believers as divided tongues of fire when they were baptized on Pentecost: "Then there appeared to them divided tongues, as of fire, and one sat upon each of them. And they were all filled with the Holy Spirit and began to speak with other tongues, as the Spirit gave them utterance" (Acts 2:3-4).

But the truth is, none of these passages from Romans, Mark, Galatians, and Acts should be used to teach the mode of baptism. We are guilty of misusing the Scriptures if we do.

Furthermore, to be "put under" water (immersion) in the Bible usually symbolized destruction, not purification. Pharaoh and his army were put under water, not Israel. The people of the flood were put under water, but not Noah. Later we see that the Bible taught that Noah's baptism, maybe by the raindrops falling on their heads, symbolized our baptism (1 Pet 3:19-21). Noah was not immersed.

If you want to know how baptism must be done today, you will have to look at how it was done in the Bible. You will see various "baptisms" being done by sprinkling or pouring, with the result that a dirty thing was declared clean. It was not a literal washing like in washing a dirty head with soap and lots of water, but a ceremonial washing. A lot of water was not required. Consider a few examples:

- Exodus 29:21, "And you shall take some of the blood that is on the altar, and some of the anointing oil, and **sprinkle it on**

Aaron and on his garments, on his sons and on the garments of his sons with him; and he and his garments shall be hallowed, and his sons and his sons' garments with him."

Aaron and the other priests declared one holy (hallowed) by virtue of the sprinkling of blood.

- Leviticus 14:7, "**And he shall sprinkle it seven times on him who is to be cleansed from the leprosy,** and shall **pronounce him clean,** and shall let the living bird loose in the open field. The leper was declared clean by virtue of being sprinkled with blood.

- Numbers 19:18-19, "A clean person shall take hyssop and dip it in the water, sprinkle it on the tent, on all the vessels, on the persons who were there, or on the one who touched a bone, the slain, the dead, or a grave. **The clean person shall sprinkle the unclean** on the third day and on the seventh day; and on the seventh day he shall purify himself, wash his clothes, and bathe in water; and **at evening he shall be clean.**"

The one who touched something that was ceremonially unclean was sprinkled with water and declared ceremonially clean.

- Hebrews 9:19-21, "For when Moses had spoken every precept to all the people according to the law, he took the blood of calves and goats, with water, scarlet wool, and hyssop, and **sprinkled both the book itself and all the people, saying, 'This is the blood of the covenant which God has commanded you.'** Then likewise **he sprinkled with blood** both the tabernacle and all the vessels of the ministry."

Moses baptized many in Israel by sprinkling them with blood so that they could worship.

- Isaiah 52:15, "So shall **He sprinkle many nations**. Kings shall shut their mouths at Him; for what had not been told them they shall see, and what they had not heard they shall consider."

God promised that he would purify and baptize the nations by sprinkling. We note that in the next chapter of Isaiah, chapter 53, the one who died to make men clean appears. Isaiah detailed the work of the suffering servant. After Isaiah, Ezekiel promised the same thing.

- Ezekiel 36:25, "**Then I will sprinkle clean water on you, and you shall be clean**; I will cleanse you from all your filthiness and from all your idols."

God would make the people clean and show that they were clean by sprinkling them with water. The water itself did not make the people clean as the text seems to suggest. The symbolic water is simply tied closely to the thing it signifies, being made clean.

And since it is not the volume of the water that made the people clean, if someone were baptized by immersion, his baptism is surely valid. Unfortunately, our Baptists brothers refuse to accept baptism by sprinkling or pouring.

When we consider the mode of baptism, we must think of it this way: There is no provable example of baptism being done by immersion, only possible insinuations, (Jesus coming up out of the water does not prove he was immersed), but there are provable examples of baptism being done by sprinkling or pouring. And if we think about it, we will find that sprinkling is much more appropriate for a newborn covenant child than immersion.

Baptism is More Than a Sign

Some see baptism as being purely a sign of the covenant of grace. To them, baptism is merely a reminder of what Christ has done for sinners. But historical Christianity has always insisted that baptism was more than a sign. Historical Christianity saw baptism as a sign and seal of the covenant of grace, just as circumcision was to Old Testament saints, like how Paul says in Romans 4:11: "And [Abraham] received the sign of circumcision, a seal of the righteousness of the faith which he had while still uncircumcised, that he might be the father of all those who believe, though they are uncircumcised, that righteousness might be imputed to them also."

The seal, which is God's mark on us, means that God owns us. We are his property. That seal is impressed on our souls every day.

So, when we receive baptism, and we do so by faith, our baptism nourishes our souls. Baptism becomes a means of strengthening (not saving) grace in our hearts. God knows man is weak and wants to reassure him, remind him, and guarantee that he is the property of the Lord.

Errors Refuted: Covenant and Baptism

- Error: Children can't repent, so they are still in their sins.

So how do we answer our Baptist and other evangelical brothers who say that children can't be forgiven without their repentance, and therefore they ought not to be baptized? We say that forgiveness of sins is God's gift to us. It is not based on what we say but it is based on what Jesus did for us. Forgiveness and repentance are gifts of God. To prove this point, suppose we did not confess all our sins before we died, does that mean that we will be lost in hell forever? Certainly not! **Everyone dies with unconfessed sins, even sins of ignorance, but none of God's children can ever be lost**. Even so, Christian children get their forgiveness through Christ's work, not through their own work. Yes, we should confess all our sins as often as we sin, but we rest in Christ's work for our forgiveness and for our salvation, not in our confession of our sins. We confess our sins because God has regenerated us.

And remember, if God condemned children through their parents without their consent, why couldn't he save children through their parents' faith without their consent if they died in infancy or are otherwise unable to exercise faith?

- Error: Some children turn out to be wicked, so none of them should be baptized as infants.

When a minister says, "people of God," does he refer to every single person in the Church? Of course not! The Church is never the "elected" ones only. The Church is God's covenant people. There are hypocrites in the Church. There will always be hypocrites in the Church as long as we are on this side of eternity. Israel was called "people of God." We remember how sinful they were at times. **Similarly, you can** rightly say in general that covenant children are God's children, though some may turn out to be wicked.

Further, Apostle Paul assumes children of believers are good and able to do good things, like truly obeying their parents from their hearts, observe: "'Honor your father and mother,' which is the first commandment with promise: 'that it may be well with you and you may live long on the earth'" (Eph 6:2-3).

And remember, **for a work to be good, it must be done from faith in Christ, according to the law of Christ, and for the glory of Christ**. So, when the Apostle Paul pointed out that children can please God, he surely was telling the truth. Take note of another verse to prove that children of believers are able to do good. This was also by the Apostle Paul: "Children, obey your parents in all things, for this is well pleasing to the Lord" (Col 3:20). Does it sound like the Apostle Paul was referring to pagans here? No. He was referring to children of God who were able to please him.

Covenant People: Whole Families

Covenant children are Christ's children, and ought to be baptized. God treats covenant children as different, and marked them by a covenant sign as they joined the Church. Throughout the Scriptures, from Abraham to the Lord Jesus, and to his disciples after him, they all treated believers' children as being distinct from children of non-believers. God marked those children by the sign of the covenant. Treating them as his children and as holy is not presumptuous.

What a precious promise baptism is to us and our children: Jesus will save us and our household. It is a gift we receive by faith. But this precious mark came at a great price. The Lord Jesus had to have his blood flow to the ground for us. This is the message that must go to our hearts and the hearts of our children.

What a comfort it is to know that our children were marked by the Lord. He singled us out for salvation. He didn't need to; he needs nothing. And then he brought our children into the covenant community.

We are the chosen of God, but we are not the "frozen chosen," as pastors often say. We have to spread the warmth of Christ's love so others may see Christ in us and be drawn to him.

Chapter 9

Sabbath Day of Worship and

Rest

Some people simply don't want to honor the Sabbath Day anymore. They believe it is valid, but they have no willingness to honor it. They have even become arrogant about their Sabbath breaking. They prefer to use it as a day of recreation, not as a day of worship and rest. Many have probably heard the line in the TV commercial, "Sunday was made for football." Others say that Sunday is "my day." This arrogance in Sabbath breaking has even entered into the Church. Surely it is bad to blatantly ignore the Sabbath, but it is worse when we know it is wrong to ignore the Sabbath and still do so.

Others, including some theologians and apologists, think that the Sabbath was only for Israel and therefore it is no longer valid. In this chapter we will first examine the evidence for the continuation of the Sabbath, we will see why we need the Sabbath, and we will touch on the method of keeping the Sabbath holy.

Why Do Many Argue That the Sabbath Is No Longer Valid?

There are some who use an argument based on the ceremonial

law to teach that the Sabbath is no longer valid. They join the Sabbath together with the other Old Testament feast days (parts of the ceremonial system), and then argue that all feasts days have been abolished. They quote the Apostle Paul to support their view: "let no one judge you in food or in drink, or regarding a festival or a new moon or sabbaths" (Col 2:16). However, a careful examination of this verse shows that the Apostle Paul was not referring to the seventh day Sabbath (the fourth commandment), but he was referring to a variety of other feasts days and special sabbaths. These sabbaths were part of the ceremonial system that indeed were fulfilled in Jesus, and are no longer valid. **When we hear of sabbaths we must not automatically think of the special seventh day of rest in the fourth commandment**. All sabbaths were not of equal value, and all sabbaths did not refer to the same thing; for example, there are at least five types of general "elder" mentioned in the Bible, but there is one specific "elder" who is a ruler in the church.

Others argue that the Sabbath is no longer valid by using an argument based on the moral law. They teach that Jesus fulfilled the Ten Commandments for us, so we are no longer under any obligation to keep the law. But will they argue that we are under no obligation to keep the other nine commandments? Of course they don't argue that. **We answer them in this way: we are not free to abuse God's name because Jesus kept the law for us, nor are we free to commit adultery because Jesus obeyed the law perfectly for us**. Jesus said that his laws, all of his moral laws, continue forever—"do not think that I came to destroy the Law or the Prophets. I did not come to destroy but to fulfill. For assuredly, I say to you, till heaven and earth pass away, one jot or one tittle will by no means pass from the law till all is fulfilled" (Matt 5:17-18).

Having Christ's righteousness counted as ours (justification) does not remove the moral obligation to obey all ten of the commandments.

The Sabbath Was a Creation Ordinance That Cannot Pass Away

There were 3 creation ordinances: keeping the Sabbath, marriage, and having children. These, by virtue of when they were given, must necessarily continue as long as we are on this earth.

God's Word teaches us that God rested on the seventh day after six days of creating: "thus the heavens and the earth, and all the host of them, were finished. And on the seventh day God ended His work which He had done, and He rested on the seventh day from all His work which He had done." (Gen 2:1-2).

It was not necessary for God to take six days to create the world, and it certainly was not necessary for God to rest on the seventh day. He had no need of rest. He never gets tired. **The only reason God said that he rested on the seventh day was to teach man of man's need to rest on the Sabbath.**

The Sabbath Was Used Before the Law Was Given to Moses at Sinai

The Lord specifically mentioned that the fourth commandment was merely a reminder of what Israel had before. All ten of the commandments were there before, but the fourth is specifically mentioned as existing before. Consider a unique example in Exodus 16. There God warned Israel to store up twice the daily amount of manna the day before the Sabbath Day. God would only have done this if the Sabbath were already understood and in force. God gave this instruction just after Israel left Egypt, and before they reached Sinai to get the codified law. Moses writes,

> And so it was, on the sixth day, that they gathered twice
> as much bread, two omers for each one. And all the rulers
> of the congregation came and told Moses. Then he said to
> them, 'This is what the LORD has said: 'Tomorrow is a
> Sabbath rest, a holy Sabbath to the LORD. Bake what
> you will bake today, and boil what you will boil; and lay

up for yourselves all that remains, to be kept until morning'" (Ex 16:22-23).

Israel saw what would happen if they did not honor the Sabbath. If they gathered more manna than they needed on the other days, it turned into worms. But if they obeyed God and gathered double the manna on the day before the Sabbath it did not turn into worms.

There are some who argue that this incident in Exodus 16 could have been post-Sinai, so it took place after the law was given. Based on the timeframe in the text, it seems that that is an unlikely possibility. Even if it were, we must remember that the Lord specifically used the term "remember," in the fourth commandment, pointing to a previously understood law.

The main point is this: **This Sabbath was not one of the ceremonial feast days, but an established moral law of God that continues to the end of the world**.

Sabbath Breaking Was One of the Reasons the Jews Were Sent into Captivity

Along with idolatry and the abusing of the widows, orphans, and foreigners, Sabbath breaking became one of the reasons for the punishment of the Jews in the Old Testament. Look at an example of God's warning to Israel, the 10 ½ tribes in the north, who were guilty of Sabbath breaking and later taken into captivity by Assyria in 722BC. He says in Amos 8:4-9,

> **Hear this, you who swallow up the needy, and make the poor of the land fail, saying: 'When will the New Moon be past, that we may sell grain? And the Sabbath, that we may trade wheat?** Making the ephah small and the shekel large, falsifying the scales by deceit, that we may buy the poor for silver, and the needy for a pair of sandals — even sell the bad wheat?' The LORD has sworn by the pride of Jacob: 'surely I will never forget

any of their works. Shall the land not tremble for this, and everyone mourn who dwells in it? All of it shall swell like the River, heave and subside like the River of Egypt. And it shall come to pass in that day,' says the Lord GOD, 'that I will make the sun go down at noon, and I will darken the earth in broad daylight.

Then the 1 ½ tribes (Judah and some of Benjamin) in the south didn't learn from the Northern Kingdom's mistake, committing the same sin. They ended up in captivity in Babylon for Sabbath breaking, among other sins.

'Thus says the LORD: **'Take heed to yourselves, and bear no burden on the Sabbath day, nor bring it in by the gates of Jerusalem; nor carry a burden out of your houses on the Sabbath day, nor do any work, but hallow the Sabbath day, as I commanded your fathers**. But they did not obey nor incline their ear, but made their neck stiff, that they might not hear nor receive instruction. And it shall be, if you heed Me carefully,' says the LORD, 'to bring no burden through the gates of this city on the Sabbath day, but hallow the Sabbath day, to do no work in it" (Jer 17:21-24).

You can understand Nehemiah's furor that even after God punished the Jews and sent them into Babylonian captivity for Sabbath breaking, they still broke the Sabbath law after they returned home. They treated the Sabbath with contempt:

'Did not your fathers do thus, and did not our God bring all this disaster on us and on this city? Yet you bring added wrath on Israel by profaning the Sabbath.' So it was, at the gates of Jerusalem, as it began to be dark before the Sabbath, that I commanded the gates to be shut, and charged that they must not be opened till after the Sabbath. Then I posted some of my servants at the gates, so that no burdens would be brought in on the Sabbath day (Neh 13:18-19).

The Sabbath Continued in the New Testament

When the Lord Jesus was on earth he honored the Sabbath. He had to. He came to obey the law for his children who had broken it. If Jesus did not keep the Sabbath, we would still be guilty of Sabbath breaking. **Further, Jesus regularly had interactions with the Jews about the Sabbath. He gave directions as to how it could be properly observed**. Jesus never attempted to invalidate the Sabbath; **Jesus simply attempted to correct the Jewish misuse of it**, like in Matthew 12:1-5:

> At that time Jesus went through the grainfields on the Sabbath. And His disciples were hungry, and began to pluck heads of grain and to eat. And when the Pharisees saw it, they said to Him, 'Look, Your disciples are doing what is not lawful to do on the Sabbath!' But He said to them, 'Have you not read what David did when he was hungry, he and those who were with him: how he entered the house of God and ate the showbread which was not lawful for him to eat, nor for those who were with him, but only for the priests? **Or have you not read in the law that on the Sabbath the priests in the temple profane the Sabbath, and are blameless?**'

Jesus performed many healings on the Sabbath, like in Matthew 12:1-12. These confirmed the existence of the Sabbath and helped to clarify the proper use of it.

The Lord threatened to punish those who taught others to not observe the Sabbath. Look at the strong words Jesus used in the Sermon on the Mount: "whoever therefore breaks one of the least of these commandments, and teaches men so, shall be called least in the kingdom of heaven; but whoever does and teaches them, he shall be called great in the kingdom of heaven" (Matt 5:19).

The Lord never taught the abrogation of the Sabbath in his three-and-a-half-year ministry on earth. This is an argument from silence, but when we take it with all the other evidences, it makes sense. **The Lord** even expected that the Sabbath would continue after he left the world when Christians would be forced to flee Jerusalem, as we see Jesus's words here: "pray that your flight may not be in winter or on the Sabbath" (Matt 24:20).

Whether we understand Matthew 24:1-35 to refer to the destruction of Jerusalem or the end of the world, the Lord Jesus clearly expected the continuation of the Sabbath. This is not an insignificant proof.

The Sabbath Continued in the New Testament with the Day Changed

The New Testament teaches that the Sabbath was changed to the first day of the week. This was a command by example. It is true that we do not imitate everything we see in the Bible, but there are a number of reasons we believe we are commanded to hold Sunday as the Christian Sabbath.

After his resurrection from the dead, Jesus met with his disciples on Sunday when they were gathered together. Look at this first time he met with them after his resurrection: "then, the same day at evening, being the first day of the week, when the doors were shut where the disciples were assembled, for fear of the Jews, Jesus came and stood in the midst, and said to them, 'Peace be with you'" (John 20:19).

Meeting with Jesus was a picture of the Church gathering to worship. Yes, this was a closed-door meeting, but this was from fear. Their doors should have been opened. Then eight days later, on the next Sunday, he met with them again in John 20:26—"after eight days His disciples were again inside, and Thomas with them. Jesus came, the doors being shut, and stood in the midst, and said, 'Peace to you!'"

It became standard practice for the disciples to meet together on the first day of the week, Sunday, after the resurrection. Even after Jesus went back to heaven the disciples continued to gather for worship on the Christian Sabbath, Sunday. We see this in Acts 20:7, where Luke reports "on the first day of the week, when the disciples came together to break bread, Paul, ready to depart the next day, spoke to them and continued his message until midnight." Luke literally said:

"On the first, the Sabbath" (Greek: *sabbaton*). Our translation ignores "sabbaton" choosing to translate the meaning rather than the word.

Now when the disciples came together to break bread, it did not mean that they came to have dinner together. Not at all! It meant that they came together for worship, and part of their worship was the celebration of the Lord's Supper. What we can conclude is that the Apostles continued the principle of remembering and honoring the resurrection of Jesus Christ (our re-creation), by meeting on Sunday instead of Saturday.

We see the Church continuing to meet and worship on Sundays, years after Jesus's ascension. We see an example of this when the Apostle Paul gave instruction for the collection of alms for the poor in Jerusalem in 1 Corinthians 16:1-2, "Now concerning the collection for the saints, as I have given orders to the churches of Galatia, so you must do also: On the first day of the week let each one of you lay something aside, storing up as he may prosper, that there be no collections when I come." Paul literally said: "On the first, the Sabbath." Our translation ignores "sabbaton." The Corinthians were called to collect offerings for poor Christians in Jerusalem when they gathered on Sunday.

The Apostle John, one of the last Apostles to die, worshipped on Sunday and was given the Revelation of Jesus Christ on Sunday, the Sabbath: "I was in the Spirit on the Lord's Day, and I heard behind me a loud voice, as of a trumpet" (Rev 1:10). History confirms, by those who lived at the same time as John, that the "Lord's Day" was Sunday.

One of the main reasons, and probably one of the most remarkable reasons for accepting Sunday as the Christian Sabbath, is found in the Old Testament. We can see how God planned for the new Sabbath to be on Sunday in the three major feasts of the Old Testament. So, the change to Sunday was not a surprise, or at least it should not have been a surprise. All three of those feasts were on Sunday, not Saturday, the usual Sabbath day.

The Feast of the Unleavened Bread, which came right after the Passover, pictured Christ's work for sinners. It was a reminder that Jesus was the Bread of Life. The Feast of the Unleavened Bread was celebrated on Sunday, as Moses said, "on the fifteenth day of the same month is the Feast of Unleavened Bread to the LORD; seven days you must eat unleavened bread" (Lev 23:6). **Day 1 of the first month was a Sabbath, so day 15 would be the day after the Old Testament Sabbath, which is Sunday**.

The Feast of Pentecost (sometimes called the Feast of Weeks or the Harvest Feast) pictured the giving of new life to the Church through the working of the Holy Spirit. Look at the details in Leviticus 23:10-11: "Speak to the children of Israel, and say to them: 'When you come into the land which I give to you, and reap its harvest, then you shall bring a sheaf of the firstfruits of your harvest to the priest. He shall wave the sheaf before the LORD, to be accepted on your behalf; on the day after the Sabbath the priest shall wave it'" (Lev 23:6). Or consider Leviticus 23:15-16, "And you shall count for yourselves from the day after the Sabbath, from the day that you brought the sheaf of the wave offering: seven Sabbaths shall be completed. Count fifty days to the day after the seventh Sabbath; then you shall offer a new grain offering to the LORD." **Fifty days after the Sabbath is Sunday—seven weeks plus one would put this feast on Sunday**. In the New Testament we see this feast of new life fulfilled when the Holy Spirit came. **Pentecost, in the New Testament, took place on Sunday, 50 days after the resurrection**.

The Feast of the Ingathering (Tabernacles) pictured the gathering of all the elect of God into Christ's kingdom. This pictures the work of the Father. It is revealed in Leviticus 23:34 and 36:

> Speak to the children of Israel, saying: 'The fifteenth day of this seventh month shall be the Feast of Tabernacles for seven days to the LORD. For seven days you shall offer an offering made by fire to the LORD. **On the eighth day you shall have a holy convocation, and you shall offer an offering made by fire to the LORD.** It is a sacred assembly, and you shall do no customary work on it.

As with the other two feasts, with 28 days in a month (lunar month), the Feast of the Ingathering was celebrated on a Sunday. **So, we can see that each of these three major feasts, which pictured the work of God redeeming his people, was on the first day of the week, Sunday**.

There is a problem for those who argue that the Sabbath continues on Saturday today, (and it is quite an interesting argument). If the Sabbath had to be celebrated on the Saturday, and since the disciples were also worshipping on Sunday on a regular basis, it would mean they were erring by taking two days off, whereas, we are commanded to work for six, not for five days. But of course this is not the main argument in support of the day change.

While the Lord never changed his Sabbath law, neither could he do so, the change in the day of the Sabbath was done in order to honor the resurrection of Jesus Christ. After Jesus returned to heaven, the churches that were formed met regularly for worship on Sundays.

The Sabbath Continued After the New Testament

Numerous early Church fathers stated that Sunday was the Christian Sabbath. Even those who were contemporaries of the Gospel writers described Sunday as the Christian Sabbath. Ignatius, one of the most ancient Church fathers said: "Let everyone that loves Christ keep holy the first day of the week, the Lord's Day." There is strong extra-biblical support for the change of day of the Sabbath from Saturday to Sunday.

The Necessity of the Sabbath

It was Commanded

Any argument against any law is settled when God commands it. We are commanded to keep the Sabbath by implication from the Garden of Eden. That command was put in written form at Mount Sinai, when

God gave Moses the Ten Commandments, specifically in Exodus 20.6-11,

> Remember the Sabbath day, to keep it holy. Six days you shall labor and do all your work, but the seventh day is the Sabbath of the LORD your God. In it you shall do no work: you, nor your son, nor your daughter, nor your male servant, nor your female servant, nor your cattle, nor your stranger who is within your gates. For in six days the LORD made the heavens and the earth, the sea, and all that is in them, and rested the seventh day. Therefore the LORD blessed the Sabbath day and hallowed it.

The Sabbath continued after Moses to the coming of Jesus. It continued during the time of Jesus. The disciples observed the Sabbath after Jesus's resurrection and ascension.

Necessity of the Sabbath: We Need Rest

No one doubts the necessity of regular physical rest. Those who try to work for seven days without any rest days soon find that the cost to their bodies and their minds is quite high. According to several scientific studies, those who work (including animals) for seven days without rest, produce less overall than those who work for six days and rest for one. But why should this be a surprise? This is how God made us. He always knows what is best for us.

Necessity of the Sabbath: We Need to Worship

We all remember that famous passage from the Epistle to the Hebrews calling us together for worship:

> Let us hold fast the confession of our hope without wavering, for He who promised is faithful. And let us consider one another in order to stir up love and good works, not forsaking the assembling of ourselves together, as is the manner of some, but exhorting one another, and so much the more as you see the Day approaching (Heb 10:23-25).

When we gather together each Sabbath for worship, good preachers will bring the Gospel of Jesus and educate us how to live; sermons are for salvation and sanctification so Christ will be glorified in us. This is feeding time. We need more than snack-sized Gospel messages. We need full meals.

Along with the preaching of the Word of God we receive the sacraments. Through the sacraments our souls are nourished and we are strengthened to fight the Devil, the world, and our own flesh.

God requires prayers and offerings on the Sabbath as well. Through prayers and offerings he is glorified, and when we do them he blesses us! We see these elements in Acts 2:42, "and they continued steadfastly in the apostles' doctrine and fellowship, in the breaking of bread, and in prayers." Our Sabbath activities must deliberately cause our minds to move away from work or study.

Necessity of the Sabbath: We Need to Work for the Glory of God

We must do good for our neighbor on the Sabbath. In fact, the Sabbath should be the most productive day of the week because we earn spiritual knowledge, and we must work to store up treasures in heaven.

Specifically, we are to do works of mercy and charity to others on the Sabbath Day, like the Corinthians did, as we saw above (1 Cor 16:2).

This is why in our church we collect money for poor students in Ukraine, poor Christians in China, and for poor orphans in Latin America. We can visit someone who is lonely. We can invite a visitor to worship, or to our homes for a meal after worship. Many churches have ministries to nursing homes on the Sabbath. Others invite college students to their homes for a home-cooked meal.

We are to show mercy to those who are around us also, like our employees or spouses so they can rest as well.

Using the Sabbath Day to celebrate birthdays, anniversaries, Mother's Day, Father's Day, or anything other than what God requires robs the Sabbath of its value. The Sabbath is not a day for personal celebrations, or to draw focus on any man, regardless of how important he might be. We must use it to focus on Christ. The Sabbath is a day to celebrate the work of the Lord Jesus and all he has done for us. It is the Lord's Day, after all. So, when we visit family and friends on the Sabbath it should be to encourage and strengthen each other in Christ, or to do works of charity and mercy.

Necessity of the Sabbath: We Need to Learn to Wait for Heaven

In the first place, the Sabbath rest draws us back to the things the Lord has done for us. The Sabbath therefore makes us meditate on God's goodness. It has always been intended for this: "remember that you were a slave in the land of Egypt, and the LORD your God brought you out from there by a mighty hand and by an outstretched arm; therefore the LORD your God commanded you to keep the Sabbath day" (Deut 5:15).

We are to remember our deliverance from our past conditions. If we forget to make the Sabbath holy we are forgetting our creation and our salvation (re-creation) in Jesus Christ.

Second, the Sabbath points us to heaven, where we will enjoy the eternal Sabbath rest. Hebrews 4:9-11 plainly says this: "There remains therefore a rest for the people of God. For he who has entered His rest has himself also ceased from his works as God did from His. Let us therefore be diligent to enter that rest, lest anyone fall according to the same example of disobedience." This is a motivation to properly keep the Sabbath holy now.

When we consider how much we need the Sabbath, we can see why God commands an end to commerce—doing unnecessary business—on the Sabbath. He wants us to focus on that which is more important, that which brings glory to him, and that which has more lasting value to us. In fact, we are to avoid all unnecessary work.

Preparation for the Sabbath

<u>**We need to prepare for the Sabbath**</u>. The word "holy" comes from the verb "to hallow." This means we are to make the Sabbath Day holy by our actions. The sky doesn't change on Sundays. The sun rises and sets. Sabbaths are cold in winter and warm in summer. It is like any other day, except for what we do. So what kind of specific actions can we take to prepare our bodies and souls for worship each Sabbath? **We must get our work done ahead of time so our minds are clear of all cares and worldly duties**. This will help us to focus on the preached Word and the holy sacraments.

Remember that the animal sacrifices in the Old Testament could not have been yoked (for work) since they wouldn't have been acceptable sacrifices to the Lord afterward. This is the same idea of our worship. We cannot come to God in worship if we are preoccupied (yoked) with work and worldly cares. God wants pure worship.

Another way of making sure we are prepared for the Sabbath is to work hard the other six days of the week. No one can truly appreciate the day of rest if he is resting for six days before. As I heard a preacher once say, "The Bible does not say that six days you shall 'loiter and do all your work,' but, 'six days you shall labor and do all your work.'"

Legalism and the Sabbath

While we are commanded to treat the Sabbath Day holy, we are not to do so in a legalistic manner. To be "legalistic" means that you make a list of "do's" and "don'ts," and demand that others follow it. That was one of the Pharisaic sins that Jesus corrected and warned against. The Sabbath is governed by principles, not a long list of restrictions and requirements. The Pharisees had more than 1600 ways in which one could break the Sabbath. They included how many steps one could walk on the Sabbath. They forbade helping the sick on the Sabbath. They forbade walking on grass, fearing that one might kick some seed from the grass and be guilty of sowing on the Sabbath. Some killed chickens for laying on the Sabbath. Legalism kills. (Poor chickens!) Remember what Jesus taught concerning the Sabbath: "He said to them, 'The Sabbath was made for man, and not man for the Sabbath'" (Mark 2:27).

Many Jews today continue these legalistic practices. Some have timers on stoves so they will turn on and off at set times so they can cook and not be guilty of "lighting fires" on the Sabbath. Some have timers on their garage doors so they don't have to open them on the Sabbath. They ignore the fact that they are using electricity from a power plant that someone else is running. Look at an example of legalism that Christ warned against:

> At that time Jesus went through the grainfields on the Sabbath. And His disciples were hungry, and began to pluck heads of grain and to eat. And when the Pharisees saw it, they said to Him, 'Look, Your disciples are doing what is not lawful to do on the Sabbath!' But He said to them, 'Have you not read what David did when he was hungry, he and those who were with him: how he entered the house of God and ate the showbread which was not lawful for him to eat, nor for those who were with him, but only for the priests? Or have you not read in the law that on the Sabbath the priests in the temple profane the Sabbath, and are blameless? Yet I say to you that in this place there is One greater than the temple. But if you had known what this means, 'I desire mercy and not sacrifice,' you would not have condemned the guiltless. For the Son of Man is Lord even of the Sabbath' (Matt 12:1-8).

Jewish legalism would have permitted someone to starve on the Sabbath. But that was not what God intended. **Legalism kills the joy of keeping the Sabbath Day holy and enjoying the picture of heaven.**

Errors Refuted: The Sabbath

- Error: I can earn more money and give to God's work if I work on the Sabbath.

I have heard at least two people say this to me. It is true that they can earn more money, but it is money earned while stealing God's time. God does not want stolen things. After all, God ordains the goals and the means for accomplishing those goals. And we must never forget that God could multiply little and make it into much, just as he used five loaves of bread and two fish to feed thousands of people. God is not desperate for more money.

- Error: I need extra money because I am struggling economically.

It is quite a strong argument when someone says: "I could lose my business if I don't work on the Sabbath." The fact is, if our business cannot make money without compromising on the Sabbath Day we need to look for another business, or another means of employment. Others might say: "Because I am poor, I could save money and get better bargains if I shopped on Sundays." Others might say: "I could get double pay if I worked on Sundays." But would God accept money from a thief? That is what the person who steals the Lord's glory on the Sabbath Day is doing. He steals God's glory so he can have more money.

Now look at the severity of the judgment that God put on those who ignored his Sabbath for reason of economics—first, individually, and then second, nationally:

Now while the children of Israel were in the wilderness, they found a man gathering sticks on the Sabbath day. And those who found him gathering sticks brought him to Moses and Aaron, and to all the congregation. They put him under guard, because it had not been explained what should be done to him. **Then the LORD said to Moses, 'The man must surely be put to death; all the congregation shall stone him with stones outside the camp.'** So, as the LORD commanded Moses, all the

congregation brought him outside the camp and stoned
him with stones, and he died (Num 15:32-36).

And then 2 Chr 36:20-21:

> And those who escaped from the sword he carried away
> to Babylon, where they became servants to him and his
> sons until the rule of the kingdom of Persia, to fulfill the
> word of the LORD by the mouth of Jeremiah, until the
> land had enjoyed her Sabbaths. As long as she lay desolate
> she kept Sabbath, to fulfill seventy years.

On the other hand, if we trusted God and obeyed him, he would bless
what we have and give us peace in our hearts, even though we don't have
all we want.

- Error: Romans 14:5 and Colossians 2:16-17 teach that to keep or
  not keep the Sabbath is my choice.

Let us look at those two verses again.

- Romans 14:5, "One person esteems one day above another;
  another esteems every day alike. Let each be fully convinced in
  his own mind."

- Colossians 2:16-17, "So let no one judge you in food or in drink,
  or regarding a festival or a new moon or sabbaths, which are a
  shadow of things to come, but the substance is of Christ."

The context of those passages disproves the idea that Christians are
somehow free from the obligation to keep the Sabbath. But first, let us
consider the words of Apostle Paul. Is he really saying the Sabbath is
passé? In the Romans passage the context was not whether to keep the
weekly Sabbath or not. The context was dealing with the weaker brother
and with the liberty that Christians have in Christ. Specifically, some ate
vegetables, some ate meat, and some preferred to keep some feast days
from the Jewish ceremonial system, while others didn't. Paul then wrote
this verse to show that Christians were given liberty concerning these
ceremonial laws. But there is no such liberty concerning the ten laws
(commandments). No one was ever free to break any of the ten moral
laws. Jesus subjected himself to all of the ten laws and never broke a
single one! In fact, Jesus had to keep all ten laws so we would get his
perfect righteousness counted as ours!

The Colossians passage is similar to the Romans passage. The context was Christian liberty from Jewish ceremonies. The Jews could maintain certain traditional days (Hanukkah, etc. if they wanted), but they could not impose those celebrations on Gentiles Christians. **Paul was protecting the liberty of the Gentile Christians. He was not saying the Sabbath was open for debate.**

Rest on the Lord's Day

It is also interesting that the fourth commandment is the longest one. With nothing happening by accident, the Lord surely knew that man needed more detailed instructions regarding this law. Even in the second rendering of the law in Deuteronomy, we find an even greater explanation regarding the fourth commandment.

What specific instructions do we have from the Lord regarding the fourth commandment? We are to keep it without fail, and we must teach others under our charge to obey it.

We keep it by resting and worshipping the Lord, even while working hard the other six days of the week. If we do, we will receive many blessings in this life and in the next. If we don't, we will bring curses on our heads, our families, our church, and our nation. This means we must guard against things that might take our focus away from our duty regarding the Sabbath.

The only thing that would make us want to keep this law is when we have rest on the inside, even in our souls, when we know that the Lord Jesus has removed all our sins and that we will have eternal rest in heaven.

Chapter 10

How Shall We Worship

We who trust in Christ for our salvation sometimes struggle to worship the true and living God as we ought. Sometimes we don't want to worship the true and living God. Often we don't know how to worship him. So, God had to give us motivation and instruction to worship. This is what we will briefly see in this chapter.   First, we will have to examine some background issues in order to be able to understand how to worship God properly.

God Wants to Be Worshipped

For sure, God needs nothing from us, whether we are believers or not. God is all-sufficient. This means he is not dependent on man for anything. Knowing that God needs nothing from us changes how we approach worship. If God needed something from us, we would have the upper hand. Hear what God says about himself: "every beast of the forest is Mine, and the cattle on a thousand hills. I know all the birds of the mountains, and the wild beasts of the field are Mine. If I were hungry, I would not tell you; for the world is Mine, and all its fullness" (Psa 50:10-12). God does not need us. We need God. **We do not add to God's nature by our worship.**

God Demands Worship

While God does not need worship, God demands our worship. And while we can say generally that we worship God through our daily lives, God calls us to worship him in a particular way. But if God doesn't need our worship, why does he require that we worship him in a particular way? When we worship God, we cause other men to praise him. When we worship God it forms a basis for God rewarding us, and these blessings are in this life and in the life to come. When we worship we are taught how to live and serve God. Psalm 50:14-15 says "offer to God thanksgiving, And pay your vows to the Most High. Call upon Me in the day of trouble; I will deliver you, and you shall glorify Me." **In Psalm 50:10-12, we noticed that after God said he needed nothing from his people, he then promptly called them to worship him**. And we must remember that God is not our brother in the sky, but is the holy, eternal, all-powerful, and just God of the entire world. This means we must come before our God with awe and adoration.

God Demands Proper Worship

God not only demands worship, he demands proper worship. From the beginning of the world we see that God required proper worship. We see God's demand for proper worship by his explicit instructions in this matter, and we also see his demand for proper worship by his disdain for improper worship.

We must not come with tiredness, and we must not come to him with sin in our hearts. If we come to worship with a grudge against our neighbor…or husband…or wife…or children, will God hear our worship? If our minds are overrun by work, how can we worship properly? **We must fix everything that hinders our worship**. Jesus said "if you bring your gift to the altar, and there remember that your brother has something against you, leave your gift there before the altar, and go your way. First be reconciled to your brother, and then come and offer your gift" (Matt 5:23-24), and also "the hour is coming, and now is, when the true worshipers will worship the Father in spirit and truth; for the

Father is seeking such to worship Him. God is Spirit, and those who worship Him must worship in spirit and truth" (John 4:23-24).

For worship to be proper, it has to be done only through the merits of Jesus's sacrifice for us. This means that only a Christian can worship the true and living God.

Consider also Cain's worship that was rejected, and Abel's worship that was accepted. Cain knew better but didn't do what God required. How do we know that Cain knew better? Look at the text: "So the LORD said to Cain, 'Why are you angry? And why has your countenance fallen? If you do well, will you not be accepted? And if you do not do well, sin lies at the door. And its desire is for you, but you should rule over it'" (Gen 4:6-7). From the phrase "if you do well," we can conclude that Cain knew better but he refused to do it. He simply refused to do well, choosing to blame God for his rejected offering.

Later God called Abraham from Ur of the Chaldees to worship him, and he did so properly. We remember how Abraham did not kill his son, Isaac, but instead worshipped God through the ram, the picture of the sacrifice of Jesus. Abraham incorporated all those who were of his household into a Church through the covenant sign of circumcision. All those who gathered in this Church worshipped through Jesus. Remember, circumcision was a picture of Christ's crucifixion. Jesus is called "our circumcision" by virtue of his death to make us clean.

After Israel was liberated from Egyptian slavery, God demanded proper worship from them. We see God's demand for proper worship through implication. He destroyed Aaron's sons who brought improper worship to him: "Then Nadab and Abihu, the sons of Aaron, each took his censer and put fire in it, put incense on it, and offered profane fire before the LORD, which He had not commanded them. So fire went out from the LORD and devoured them, and they died before the LORD" (Lev 10:1-2).

Later, as Israel travelled through the desert to Canaan, we see God's demands for proper worship when he gave the details of the construction of the tabernacle, and directions for proper worship. **God was uncompromising in his directions for his worship**. In Exodus 30:8-9 he particularly warned against anyone offering inappropriate offerings on his altar, saying "when Aaron lights the lamps at twilight, he shall burn incense on it, a perpetual incense before the LORD throughout your generations. You shall not offer strange incense on it, or a burnt offering, or a grain offering; nor shall you pour a drink offering on it."

Look at some more notable examples of God's demand for proper worship when the tabernacle was being built. Everything had to be built, furnished, and used exactly as God said.

- Exodus 25:9, "According to all that I show you, that is, the pattern of the tabernacle and the pattern of all its furnishings, just so you shall make it."
- Exodus 25:40, "And see to it that you make them according to the pattern which was shown you on the mountain."
- Exodus 29:35, "Thus you shall do to Aaron and his sons, according to all that I have commanded you. Seven days you shall consecrate them."
- Exodus 30:37, "But as for the incense which you shall make, you shall not make any for yourselves, according to its composition. It shall be to you holy for the LORD."

Anyone departing from God's demands was met with God's anger and justice. After Israel entered Canaan, God continued to demand proper worship. He rejected Eli's sons for corrupting worship and for living corrupt lives that frustrated those who worshipped him.

Later, God rejected King Saul because he corrupted the worship of God by taking on an authority that God did not give to him. He took on the office of a priest, an office that was not given to him.

Finally, one of the main reasons for the Assyrian and Babylonian captivities was Israel's and Judah's ignoring of worship altogether. The Sabbath Day became a burden on their heads. Many brought polluted sacrifices to God. Others made proper sacrifices, but did not have the right heart in worship. So God rejected their worship.

Does God Have the Right to Determine How People Worship?

God has a right to determine how we are to worship him because he is our Creator. We have no need for another reason, but we do have another reason. **God is our re-creator in Jesus Christ.** That plan to save us through Jesus started a long time ago. Jesus was the ground by which men were brought into the church in the OT and NT. We were purchased with his own blood, as Paul said, "therefore take heed to yourselves and to all the flock, among which the Holy Spirit has made you overseers, to shepherd the church of God **which He purchased with His own blood** (Acts 20:28).
Since you belong to him, body and soul, he has the absolute right to demand worship and to demand how we are to worship him.

How Do We Worship God?

How do we worship God in a way that he finds acceptable? Principally, we worship God according to his law. We can see regulations for worship in the first four commandments.

We must worship God and God alone. This is the point of the first law. It is a high sin to worship God while worshipping other gods alongside him. Those who attempt this will find God a God of vengeance. This is what is often called a "Christian" sin, as it is a sin committed by those who believe. Christians know and believe in the one God, yet at times they have other gods alongside him. The non-believer does not know the one true God personally. This is why the Christian sin of worshipping another god alongside God is worse. We know better.

We must worship God without the use of any idols. This second commandment or law is really the center of where we look for directions of how to worship God. The intention of this law is that we must not worship God with any human inventions, idols being the worst invention.

We must worship God with proper reverence. So, we must not misuse the name of the Lord ever. To do that is to abuse his person, as the name represents the person.

We must worship God on the Sabbath corporately with other believers. Though we may worship God on other days, they are not commanded. We must worship on the Sabbath. Though we may worship God privately, and though we may worship as families, and if fact, we are commanded to do so, we must worship with the people of God each Sabbath. Remember what the writer of Hebrews wrote:

> Let us hold fast the confession of our hope without wavering, for He who promised is faithful. And let us consider one another in order to stir up love and good works, not forsaking the assembling of ourselves together, as is the manner of some, but exhorting one another, and so much the more as you see the Day approaching. For if we sin willfully after we have received the knowledge of the truth, there no longer remains a sacrifice for sins, but a certain fearful expectation of judgment, and fiery indignation which will devour the adversaries (Heb 10:23-27).

Let us now move from the principles of worship that we find in the first four commandments to the specifics of how we are to worship him. But before we do that, we must point out one more principle of worship.

Worship is Dialogical

There is no doubt that man, when he was created, was to remain close to God. We see that closeness when the Lord Jesus, in his pre-incarnate form, met with man each evening before man's fall in the Garden of Eden. That closeness was expressed in conversation. It is this same principle that we must see in worship, even as we are being restored to that right relationship with God. Talking back and forth is a dialog, hence the term "dialogical." So it is common to see dialog in worship. God speaks and then man speaks.

But we do have to be careful when we speak of worship being a dialog between God and man, especially since we talk to God outside of worship, and he speaks back to us through his Word. That is a form of worship, but that is personal worship. Now, however, we want to speak of the details and richness of our dialogical corporate worship of the one true God. Corporate worship is when the Church officially gathers for worship under the oversight of the elders.

Elements of Worship

I once heard a young man say in a church, "Let's do worship." In the first case, we don't "do" worship. We worship. But my bigger objection to what he was saying was that worship was singing. That was what he meant by "doing worship." **But singing is not worship. Singing is a part of worship.** Closing our eyes with uplifted hands is not what God meant when he called his people to worship him.

So, what are the elements of worship? In short, worship is listening to the preaching of the Word of God, giving and receiving the sacraments, praying, and singing. (Taking of vows before God is properly part of worship, but that is an occasional element.) It is interesting that while singing now is considered the primary part of worship in many churches, historically, sometimes when the Church met there was little singing. Worship was often called "Word and sacraments," to emphasize the preaching and the picturing of the Gospel, like we see in Acts 2:42: "and they continued steadfastly in the apostles' doctrine and fellowship, in the breaking of bread, and in prayers."

Luke, the writer of the Book of Acts, wrote of the three main elements of worship. "The apostle's doctrine," was preaching. "Breaking of bread" was representative of the sacraments. And of course we see prayers included. Singing is not mentioned, as it was likely understood. We cannot help but sing the praises of God. God even gave us a book full of songs with a command to sing them all (the Psalms). **In dialogical worship God speaks by preaching and in the sacraments.** (The sacraments are a visible sermon about the work of

Jesus on the cross.) **Man responds to God through prayer and singing**.

Now in order to accomplish this task of properly worshipping God the Reformers returned to an order of worship, sometimes called a liturgy. All elements of the liturgy ensure that worship is proper (according to the first four commandments), and that inappropriate elements are prevented from entering in worship.

Practical Application of the Elements of Worship

The minister, God's representative, calls the congregation to worship. This is often done by reading a verse or a few verses that draw the worshipper's attention to the call of God to worship him.

The minister then reminds us why we come to worship. A minister might say, for instance, "Brothers and sisters in Jesus Christ, our help is in the name of the Lord our God who made heaven and earth." This draws the believer to the greatness of God (he made heaven and earth.) and the goodness of God (we go to him for help with our physical and spiritual needs.). In some congregations, the congregation, not the minister, might confess that their "help is in the name of the Lord." The Latin word for this confession, which some congregations still use in their bulletin, is "*votum*." Votum means a vow that is made to God.

The minister then shows the inside of his hand to salute the congregation; he says that God has nothing against his people who are coming to worship him, and they are therefore free to worship him. The minister might say, "Grace to you and peace from God the Father and the Lord Jesus Christ." This is often called a salutation. It is like when a junior soldier salutes a senior soldier, exposing the palm of his hands to show that he has no secret weapons against him, and then the senior solider reciprocates, showing that he has no weapon in his hand against the junior soldier. This is why a salutation is important. With the basis of approach to God in worship clear, worship can progress.

The minister leads in singing and often does so throughout the worship service. The singing is focused on the work of Christ and his redemption. The Psalms, God's primary songbook to the Church, is given the primary place in our singing. (Some congregations may have a confession of sins before singing). Singing is clearly commanded as part of worship: "let the peace of God rule in your hearts, to which also you were called in one body; and be thankful. Let the word of Christ dwell in you richly in all wisdom, teaching and admonishing one another in psalms and hymns and spiritual songs, singing with grace in your hearts to the Lord" (Col 3:15-16).

Even though the Psalms are our primary book of singing, songs which are faithful to Scripture, and which put the focus on the work of Jesus are also properly included in worship. We confidently sing faithful hymns and not Psalms only because we know there were already additional hymns that were written and sung in the Old Testament system of worship, which were not included in the Psalms. Further, we have evidence of hymns that were quite fitting for worship in other parts of the Bible, hymns like the songs of Simeon and Mary. And who would not want to sing the song of Hannah or Deborah? **Further, with the progress of revelation, we know more details about the work of redemption in the New Testament, so we have more to sing about. If we read about the details of the work of Christ in worship we can surely sing about the details of the work of Christ in worship.**

We regularly read the law of God in our worship services. Some churches may focus on one law each week. Other churches read the law from various parts of the Bible. Most would read one of the two renderings of the Ten Commandments/laws from Exodus or Deuteronomy. But why do we hear the law of God each week? We hear it for three reasons.

God's law teaches us how we may live before our God who redeemed us, and we learn how we may have hurt our Lord in the past week.

God's law teaches us how we may use it as a basis of order for our society. The law restrains evil. No society should be founded on anything but God's law. So, politicians would do well to be in church each Sunday to hear God's law explained and applied.

God's law teaches non-believers how they have broken God's law in thoughts, words, and action. This will lead them to repentance. Paul taught "by the deeds of the law no flesh will be justified in His sight, for by the law is the knowledge of sin" (Rom 3:20).

A prayer of confession often follows the reading of the law. This prayer can be a written prayer or a prayer in song form. In most churches the congregation would sing or say the prayer of confession in unison, together. In some churches the pastor may pray on behalf of the congregation. My preference is for well-written congregational prayers that we can rotate from week to week.

After the prayer of confession, the minister, the servant of God, speaks for God and declares that our sins are forgiven based on the work of Jesus on the cross, and that God will not hold against us any of our sins. We are encouraged to not let our sins or the guilt of our sins weigh us down.

Then comes the reading, explaining, and applying of the Word of God to each believer. This logically follows the declaration of pardon after the guilt of sin is removed; the major obstacle from clearly hearing God's Word is gone. In one of the two worship services on the Lord's Day, Reformed churches focus on a passage of Scripture and directly explain and apply the doctrines of Scripture. In the other worship service, we often focus on our confessional statements. Confessional statements are historical, time-tested, and accepted doctrines. These include the Heidelberg Catechism, Canons of Dort, Belgic Confession of Faith, Apostles' Creed, Athanasian Creed, Westminster Confession of Faith, and the Westminster Larger and Shorter Catechisms.

The doctrine is then examined, based on Scriptures, and applied to the lives of the hearers. The minister, as God's servant, authoritatively declares God's truth, and God requires that his people prepare to receive it. We have an unmistakable command to read the Word of God, to preach, and to listen! "Preach the word! Be ready in season and out of season. Convince, rebuke, exhort, with all longsuffering and teaching" (2 Tim 4:2), and 1 Thessalonians 5:27, "I charge you by the Lord that this epistle be read to all the holy brethren." This reflects how God has always been worshipped by faithful believers: "for Moses has had throughout many generations those who preach him in every city, being read in the synagogues every Sabbath" (Acts 15:21).

Many ministers will pray for the congregational and international Church's needs in a special prayer. This is called a congregational or pastoral prayer. I would ask the congregation to listen carefully, agree with my prayer as the pastor, and give a hearty "Amen" in the end. This becomes the prayer of the whole congregation.

Churches often allow people to give offerings for the poor and needy as well. Some may prefer an offering box at the back of the church so members can give their tithes and special offerings. Most pass an offering basket around.

Toward the end of the worship service we sing a doxology, which is a song of praise to God. Doxology literally means "glory words." We praise God for meeting with us, listening to us, and speaking to us. The most popular doxology is: "Praise God from whom all blessings flow. Praise him, all creatures here below. Praise him above, ye heavenly host. Praise Father, Son, and Holy Ghost. Amen."

The doxology is then followed by God blessing his people through the minister. This is often called a benediction. Literally it means "good words," or "blessing." The minister as God's servant is commanded to be God's agent in the pronouncement of God's blessing on the congregation. Here are two examples of the most common benedictions:

- Numbers 6:23-27 "Speak to Aaron and his sons, saying, 'This is the way you shall bless the children of Israel.' Say to them: 'The LORD bless you and keep you; the LORD make His face shine upon you, and be gracious to you; the LORD lift up His countenance upon you, and give you peace.' 'So they shall put My name on the children of Israel, and I will bless them.'"

- 2 Corinthians 13:14, "The grace of the Lord Jesus Christ, and the love of God, and the communion of the Holy Ghost, be with you all. Amen."

Some churches put the doxology after the benediction.

Who Leads Worship?

In Reformed churches, only elders and ministers lead worship. Elders and ministers lead worship because they are the ones responsible for the spiritual oversight of the congregation. They have to guard what is said and done from the pulpit for the people of God. Other members who are not elders are not permitted to lead in worship. So, women are not to lead in worship either, as they do not have spiritual authority over the congregation. New converts to the faith must not lead worship as they do not have the spiritual wisdom. Children are not to lead for the same reason. It might seem cute to allow a young child to lead in worship, and it might make his parents want to take him to church, and it might seem inclusive to ask women to lead, especially if they are highly educated, but God explicitly forbids those who were not qualified to lead worship in the Church. Remember, it is his Church, and only he determines how he is to be worshipped. Similarly, only elders are to serve the Lord's Supper, not women or children, as the elders are to guard the Lord's Table and enforce discipline.

To ensure that leadership in worship is protected and to show how precious worship is to God, God ordained that the local church provides financially for the minister who regularly leads their worship.

What About Choirs and Special Music?

There is nothing wrong with beautiful and godly music. Beautiful music is a gift of God. But when we gather for worship we do not gather as individuals. We gather as the people of God. God speaks to us and we respond to him. So the question arises: If the congregation is the choir today, why were there choirs in the Old Testament worship? Look at one example: "these are the singers, heads of the fathers' houses of the Levites, who lodged in the chambers, and were free from other duties; for they were employed in that work day and night" (1 Chr 9:33).

The answer is this: The Levites and the priests (all priests were Levites), pictured the work of the church and the Savior. The priests made sacrifices before, but we don't need priests anymore because Jesus was our sacrifice. The veil in the temple was torn from top to bottom when Jesus died on the cross. This means that all who believe in Jesus now have access to the Father in heaven. We don't need priests anymore. And the Levites, with personal preparation, sang for the Church, but now we have been prepared by the work of our High Priest, Jesus, to sing for ourselves. Peter says, "you are a chosen generation, a royal priesthood, a holy nation, His own special people, that you may proclaim the praises of Him who called you out of darkness into His marvelous light" (1 Pet 2:9).

So those who want to have representative singing (choirs) in worship are desiring to return to the Old Testament symbols, ignoring the fact that the symbols have now passed. But of course, choirs, in their proper place, can be things of beauty. (Take a listen to a good choir singing Handel's *Messiah*, if you haven't yet.)

Positively, what is more beautiful than for the whole congregation singing? Paraphrasing a pastor friend of mine: "Listen to the voices of the bass, the tenors, the sopranos, the altos, the children, and the hums of the elderly! What beautiful music we can make to our God."

What About All the Other Ceremonies of the Old Testament?

Believers in the Old Testament were in the same Church, had the same faith, had the same Savior and worshipped the same God, but before that Savior appeared in time 2,000 years ago, there were many symbols and sacrifices that represented his work. Consider some examples of Old Testament ceremonies.

Priests, who represented Jesus, were required to wear an ephod, a breastplate embedded with precious stones, and a turban. This pictured Jesus carrying and caring for all his people. The Ark of the Covenant in the Holiest Place, which had two golden angels on either side of the cover, pictured heaven and the throne from which we receive mercy. There were symbols of Jesus and of his work in the temple.

There were five major sacrifices—burnt, grain, peace, sin, and trespass offerings. These represented different aspects of the work of the Savior.

There were the three major feasts—Passover, Pentecost, and Booths. These pictured the work of the Lord Jesus, the Holy Spirit, and the Father.

The priest had to make intercessions for the people, picturing what Jesus does for us in heaven now. All this pomp and ceremony of Old Testament worship pointed to and were fulfilled in Christ's life and death on earth and his consequent return to heaven. The Old Testament worship was only a shadow of things to come, only a shadow of Jesus. When the Light of the Word appeared, the shadows had to necessarily flee. So, the shadows, the symbolic things of the Old Testament are no longer necessary or valid. Who would want to look at a photograph instead of the real person? With all the pictures and ceremonies passed, you now see simplicity in worship in the New Testament.

Errors Refuted: Worship

- Error: Women are allowed to lead in worship.

In order to answer this assertion, let us start by considering the strong language the Apostle Paul used in 1 Corinthians 14:34-35, where he said "let your women keep silent in the churches, for they are not permitted to speak; but they are to be submissive, as the law also says. And if they want to learn something, let them ask their own husbands at home; for it is shameful for women to speak in church."

The Apostle Paul asserted the same thing to Timothy, except that he spoke in more detail, saying

> In like manner also, that the women adorn themselves in
> modest apparel, with propriety and moderation, not with
> braided hair or gold or pearls or costly clothing, but,
> which is proper for women professing godliness, with
> good works. Let a woman learn in silence with all

submission. And I do not permit a woman to teach or to have authority over a man, but to be in silence. For Adam was formed first, then Eve. And Adam was not deceived, but the woman being deceived, fell into transgression (1 Tim 2:9-14).

The plain language of the text does not permit women to lead in worship.

Some don't like the fact that women are not permitted to rule or to teach, and argue pragmatically that the Church must loosen up and let women be leaders or preachers, or the Church will die. But we must run the Church the way God says. The Church belongs to God by creation and re-recreation. And we must not forget that God ordains the goals and the means to achieve those goals. Further, Jesus builds his Church, not us. If Jesus says he will build his Church, we can have confidence in him. We do not adjust his explicit instruction.

Others argue that because women are as educated as men, they should be included in leadership in the Church. The Bible never says that women were not permitted to teach because they didn't have the ability or the knowledge to teach. **God simply does not permit it by virtue of the order of creation and as part of the curse when Eve sinned first by giving in to the Devil (see 1 Timothy 2:12-13 again).** Even before the fall, Eve had neither the authority nor the qualification to lead.

Others argue that women were forbidden from leading worship during the New Testament times only because it was not culturally acceptable. The answer is simple: God's laws don't change over time to accommodate changing cultures. God's laws are permanent.

- Error: We can offer God the best we can in worship and he will accept that.

Consider what the Apostle Paul said to the church in Colossae:

Therefore, if you died with Christ from the basic principles of the world, why, as though living in the world, do you subject yourselves to regulations — 'Do not touch, do not taste, do not handle,' which all concern things which perish with the using — according to the

commandments and doctrines of men? These things
indeed have an appearance of wisdom in self-imposed
religion, false humility, and neglect of the body, but are of
no value against the indulgence of the flesh (2:20-23).

What some of the Colossians were doing was actually "will" worship.
They offered what they wanted to God. But notice how Paul
characterized their activity. Their activities even appeared to be wise but
were not wise at all.

Consider also how God showed his displeasure with
unacceptable worship in the past: consider Korah who wanted to be like
a priest during the days of Moses and how God dealt with him. We see in
Numbers 16:3, "they gathered together against Moses and Aaron, and
said to them, 'You take too much upon yourselves, for all the
congregation is holy, every one of them, and the LORD is among them.
Why then do you exalt yourselves above the assembly of the LORD?'"
And then the result: "And a fire came out from the LORD and
consumed the two hundred and fifty men who were offering incense"
(Num 16:35). God, in a dramatic way, destroyed Korah and those who
rebelled with him. This shows how strongly God felt about his worship.

Eli was indifferent about how his sons led worship! He did not
restrain them. Eli only told them to stop doing their bad deeds. Look:

Why do you kick at My sacrifice and My offering which I
have commanded in My dwelling place, and honor your
sons more than Me, to make yourselves fat with the best
of all the offerings of Israel My people?' . . . 'Behold, the
days are coming that I will cut off your arm and the arm
of your father's house, so that there will not be an old
man in your house (1 Sam 2:29, 31).

Uzza corrupted the worship of God by carrying the Ark of the
Covenant in a wrong way. He thought it was worse for the Ark to touch
the ground than to touch him. He found out differently. He reached out
and touched it and God killed him: "when they came to Chidon's
threshing floor, Uzza put out his hand to hold the ark, for the oxen

stumbled. Then the anger of the LORD was aroused against Uzza, and He struck him because he put his hand to the ark; and he died there before God" (1 Chr 13:9-10).

And who could forget King Saul who was cursed by God because he corrupted the worship by assuming the office of a priest? "Samuel said 'Has the LORD as great delight in burnt offerings and sacrifices, as in obeying the voice of the LORD? Behold, to obey is better than sacrifice, and to heed than the fat of rams. For rebellion is as the sin of witchcraft, and stubbornness is as iniquity and idolatry'" (1 Sam 15:22-23).

God killed Ananias and Sapphira for their corruption of worship, in Acts 5. They stole the money they had given for the worship of God.

God killed those who misused the Lord's Supper, as we see in 1 Corinthians 11. This warning is often repeated in our churches when we participate in the Lord's Supper.

And do you remember when Aaron made a golden calf for Israel to use in worship when Israel waited for Moses to return from the mountain? That calf was a mere representation of God, not a distant idol, but God rejected it and pronounced judgment on the wicked: "then he took the calf which they had made, burned it in the fire, and ground it to powder; and he scattered it on the water and made the children of Israel drink it" (Ex 32:20).

God wanted them to see that images of himself were worthy of nothing less than excretion, fit for the toilet. **To put it strongly, to worship God in the way we want is nothing short of idolatry, idolatry of self**.

- Error: The church, to be relevant, must be willing to accept changes in worship.

Many want change in the area of worship, trying to make it relevant, and they want to do so using the democratic process. **But the Church is not a democracy**. The Church is not a social organization like the Kiwanis Clubs. God's views are greater than the whole world's view combined. And the Church is not run by one person who might be wealthier than others in the Church. The Church is owned by God and it must serve God in a way that he sees fit.

Others want the Church to be willing to change and make it more accommodating, more inviting. While it is true that churches need to be more welcoming, and ministers must be willing to consider things like the language of the people who are attending, the regulations set by God for worship are not negotiable. (Speaking in understandable language and having the Bible in the common language are expected by God.) But for local church leaders to ignore God's commands regarding worship, and to change it to suit man's desires or his "felt needs," is to literally invite God's judgment on their people.

Worship is God's Call

Our holy God wants to be worshipped, so he restored sinful man to himself and called on his redeemed people to worship him. Worship is first and foremost for the glory of God. Our Redeemer wants to be worshipped in the way that he determined. He does not want to be worshipped the way we think is best.

Those who corrupt the worship of God can expect that he will be angry, for **God's greatest anger in the Bible is reserved for those who worshipped him in an incorrect way.**

Our worship today is simple, but profound. We would do well then to learn to worship the Lord. We must fight the urge to worship him in a way that we choose. When we worship God properly, he is pleased.

Now What?

I did not intend for this book to be an exhaustive study of any of these Reformation doctrines. These doctrines will take a lot more time to explain. And there are more skilled theologians who have taught these doctrines in greater detail. What I intend is that this little book stimulates you to study more and study widely.

So, study more. Read good theology books. Get into a faithful church. Listen to sound teaching. Many sermons are available online from places like www.sermonaudio.com. Hundreds of thousands of sermons are available on YouTube and on other online sources.

And above all else, as your knowledge increases, as you learn more of the greatness of God and the wonder of your salvation, let your love for God and your neighbor increase. **Don't let knowledge end with you.** Don't let your knowledge become a curse.

28241949R00122

Made in the USA
Lexington, KY
11 January 2019